Series / Number 07-008

W9-BQX-031
LINCOLN CHRISTIAN COLLEGE AND SEMINARY

ANALYSIS OF ORDINAL DATA

DAVID K. HILDEBRAND
University of Pennsylvania

JAMES D. LAING
University of Pennsylvania
and Stanford University

HOWARD ROSENTHAL
Carnegie-Mellon University

SAGE PUBLICATIONS
The International Professional Publishers
Newbury Park London New Delhi

Copyright © 1977 by Sage Publications, Inc.

Printed in the United States of America

All rights reserved. No part of this book may be reproduced or utilized in any form or by any means, electronic or mechanical, including photocopying, recording, or by any information storage and retrieval system, without permission in writing from the publisher.

For information address:

SAGE Publications, Inc.
2455 Teller Road
Newbury Park, California 91320
E-mail: order@sagepub.com

SAGE Publications Ltd.
6 Bonhill Street
London EC2A 4PU
United Kingdom

SAGE Publications India Pvt. Ltd.
M-32 Market
Greater Kailash I
New Delhi 110 048 India

International Standard Book Number 0-8039-0795-8

Library of Congress Catalog Card No. L.C. 77-72857

00 01 02 03 28 27 26 25 24 23

When citing a professional paper, please use the proper form. Remember to cite the correct Sage University Paper series title and include the paper number. One of the two following formats can be adapted (depending on the style manual used):

(1) IVERSEN, GUDMUND R. and NORPOTH, HELMUT (1976) "Analysis of Variance." Sage University Paper series on Quantitative Applications in the Social Sciences, 07-001. Beverly Hills and London: Sage Publications.

OR

(2) Iversen, Gudmund R. and Norpoth, Helmut. 1976. *Analysis of Variance.* Sage University Paper series on Quantitative Applications in the Social Sciences, series no. 07-001. Beverly Hills and London: Sage Publications.

CONTENTS

107948

Editor's Introduction

Ordinal data are the type of reliable information most frequently available to social scientists. Rather than simply providing information on how to *categorize* data—a function performed by analysis of nominal data*—ordinal data provide an *ordering* of cases from the highest to lowest, hottest to coldest, best to worst. Ordinals lack a unit of measurement, but permit a comparison of items so that one can determine which item is less than the other. *Ordinals are, therefore, sometimes called "comparative concepts."*

ANALYSIS OF ORDINAL DATA provides comparisons in which we can have considerable confidence—although such data are not as precise as interval data, which provide measures of how *much* higher one item is than the others. Therefore, ANALYSIS OF ORDINAL DATA will tell us with considerable assurance that one stimulus is stronger than another (but not *how much* stronger). This kind of information is valuable to:

- Experimental psychologists, who depend on ordinal data for the analysis of psychological variables—reactions to stimuli are typically expressed in precisely the terms of "more" or "less" which require techniques of ordinal data analysis.
- Sociologists, who might study status by asking respondents to rate (according to prestige) such occupations as teacher, secretary, doctor, salesman, and plumber; or who might study alienation by asking persons of differing socioeconomic backgrounds to rank their attitudes toward aspects of society.
- Political scientists, who might deal in surveys asking whether a respondent is "liberal, moderate, or conservative" on an ideological continuum.
- Economists, who frequently maintain that consumers cannot state with any degree of reliability the extent to which they prefer competing commodities, but can at least rank order their preferences.
- School administrators, who can plan programs incorporating student preferences more effectively by asking for a rating (in order of preference) to such questions as: which would you usually prefer to order if our school cafeteria served sandwiches, salads, or "blue plates" for lunch?

---

*For further discussion, see the paper in this series by H. T. Reynolds (1977) *Analysis of Nominal Data.* Sage University Papers on Quantitative Applications in the Social Sciences, series no. 07-007. Beverly Hills and London: Sage Publications.

Whenever respondents provide a basic data set that places variables in a significant order, those facts lend themselves to ANALYSIS OF ORDINAL DATA.

This paper on the ANALYSIS OF ORDINAL DATA is important partly because ordinal data are so widely used by students, teachers, and researchers in the social sciences, and partly because it applies a conceptual scheme recently developed by the authors—*prediction analysis*—to ordinal data. Their approach encompasses the more traditional ways of analyzing ordinal data presented in standard introductory texts. Hence this paper introduces readers to ANALYSIS OF ORDINAL DATA in general and to prediction analysis in particular.

ANALYSIS OF ORDINAL DATA thus presents the conventional ordinal measures of association, as well as the way in which these measures relate to one another *and* the status of these measures overall in a broad theoretical context. The commonly used ordinal measures of association are critically examined and evaluated with cautions and warnings against particular measures carefully argued and documented. The prediction analysis framework provides a viable new approach for ANALYSIS OF ORDINAL DATA.

—E. M. Uslaner, Series Editor

ANALYSIS OF ORDINAL DATA

DAVID K. HILDEBRAND
University of Pennsylvania

JAMES D. LAING
University of Pennsylvania and Stanford University

HOWARD ROSENTHAL
Carnegie-Mellon University

1. ORDINAL MEASUREMENT

Propositions stated in the form, "the more of this, the more of that," are common in social science. Another prediction style is illustrated by the statement, "If any observation is rated ***high*** on the first variable, then it tends to be ***medium*** or ***high*** on the other." Both of these statements illustrate propositions relating ordinal variables. This paper discusses ways to evaluate such propositions with scientific data.

In the following sections we discuss the ordinal measurement of variables, identify alternative types of propositions relating ordinal variables, and present methods for using data to evaluate how successfully such propositions predict observed events.

The basic strategy of this paper is to develop a general prediction framework and a related statistical measure, $\nabla_{\mathcal{P}}$. This general framework is then used to explain the most widely used measures of bivariate association for ordinal variables, including gamma and the various d and tau measures. These measures were designed to evaluate "the more of this, the more of that" type of proposition. Many other types of propositions can be evaluated with the general framework. After dealing extensively with bivariate propositions, we briefly consider the

AUTHORS' NOTE: ***We thank our research assistant, Richard Gunsaulus, for a careful and critical reading of the manuscript. We have also benefitted from comments by the series editor and a referee.***

evaluation of multivariate predictions. The general framework not only provides a common perspective for interpreting standard measures of association. When a research application arises where no standard measure is appropriate to evaluate the specific proposition of interest, the framework permits custom-designing of a measure.

Many types of variables are used in science. We can distinguish between *quantitative* and *qualitative* variables. The particular value (amount, degree, or intensity) that an observation exhibits on a quantitative variable is expressed as a (real) number. Examples of quantitative variables include temperature measured in degrees Celsius, material wealth in dollars, and a candidate's electoral support in votes. However–whether as an inherent property of the concept being measured, inadequacies in measurement techniques, or the investigator's research goals–many important concepts are measured only qualitatively.

There are two basic types of qualitative variables: nominal and ordinal. A *nominal* variable consists of a set of alternative and mutually exclusive categories or states, so that each observation is assigned to just one state. For example, a voter's home region might be described by one of the categories: *East, Midwest, South,* or *West*. The states of a nominal variable may be listed in any arbitrary order. (On analysis of nominal data, see Hildebrand, Laing, and Rosenthal, 1974a, 1974b, 1975, 1976, 1977; Reynolds, 1977.) An *ordinal* variable also has a set of mutually exclusive states. Unlike a nominal variable, however, an ordinal variable's states are ordered or ranked in terms of the alternative amounts or degrees of intensity that the states represent. For example, Aberbach and Rockman (1976) classified each member of a sample of top-level Washington bureaucrats in terms of their support for a greater government role in the provision of social services. The ordered categories or states they used were: *left* (the highest degree of support), *left-center, center, right-center,* and *right.*

For certain sets of categories, investigators impose order for theoretical reasons. Consider, for example, the three categories, *Democrat, Republican,* and *Independent*. For some purposes of analysis, these categories might be viewed as nominal. Social scientists, however, frequently impose an order, viewing *Independent* as the middle category–presumably because party affiliation is an index of preferences on the liberal-conservative dimension. One could go even further and assign numerical values to the categories, letting Democrat be 1, Independent 0, and Republican –1, or, as another possibility, Democrat 2, Independent .625, Republican 0. Typically social scientists don't go this far; although they operate as if the categories were ordered, social scientists are generally unwilling to assert that they can measure numerically the amounts of the variable represented by these categories. In fact, the Aberbach and Rockman research illustrates the typical approach; they used party affiliation as an ordinal independent (predictor) variable in the analysis of support for social services as a dependent (predicted) variable.

Ordinal variables are important for several reasons. First, at least in some situations certain concepts can only (or, at least, readily and economically) be measured at the ordinal level. For example, in grading essays, the teacher may feel confident that the quality of any essay graded A is better than any graded B, that B is better than C, and C is better than D. Yet he may be unwilling to make such quantitative judgments as, "An A paper is six times better than a C paper." Luke may be able to tell Sue with confidence that the bath water feels *hot, warm, cool,* or *cold,* but be unable to judge the water temperature accurately in degrees Celsius. (In fact, Sue might think Luke is a little strange if he gives a quantitative judgment in this situation.) Similarly, in coding interview data, researchers might believe that their judgmental capacities are only fine enough to justify using a small number of ordered categories. Again the Aberbach and Rockman study is representative: they used five ordered categories of support for social services (*left, left-center, center, right-center,* and *right*).

Second, in some situations only the ordering of observations on a quantitative variable matters; specific numerical values have no importance. For example, in professional baseball, and in many other social processes as well, relative–rather than absolute–performance is what counts. A baseball team's share of post-season monies does not depend directly on the percentage of games the team won. Rather, it depends on how the team performed relative to the other teams in the same division. Players on the first-place team get a large amount of money, those on the second-place team much less, those on the third-place team still less, and the fourth-, fifth-, and sixth-place teams get nothing. Similarly, the traditional French *agrégation* exam divided a fixed number of available teaching slots among the highest scorers on the exam, the best plums going to the best finishers. In Congress, seniority is not measured by the number of years of consecutive service but by the relative ranking of members in this regard. These examples indicate that ordinal data do not always contain less relevant information than related quantitative data. If we are told that the Phillies finished first in the National League East, we know that they won more games than any of the other five teams in that division; we would not know this if we had been told, instead, that the Phillies won 75 percent of their games. On the other hand, of course, knowing that a team finished first does not tell us what percent of games it won.

In this paper, an ordinal variable is defined simply as a set of mutually exclusive states that are ordered in terms of the characteristic of interest. Although various refinements to ordinal measurement are possible, such as ranking the distances between various states as well as ranking the states themselves, we do not consider such complications here. At times, it will be useful to give numerical names to states of an ordinal variable such as (1) high, (2) medium, (3) low. Note that, when the ordering is a rating or ranking, we use low numbers to indicate high ratings. This conforms to a cultural convention that "high ranks" are assigned "low numbers": the team winning the greatest number of games is "number one." Thus, the lower the number used to index the state, the greater the "amount" of the variable that the state represents. It is important to recognize that the purpose of these numeric names is only to indicate the rank of the variable state in the ordering; no additional significance should be attached to these numbers. In fact, any set of numeric state labels that assigns the same order to the states will serve equally well. For example, suppose that no two teams in the National League East had identical won-lost records. Then we may use the numbers [1, 2, 3, 4, 5, 6] to indicate the ranking of the six teams in the final division standings. These particular numbers are convenient, since "3" means "finished in third place," and so on. Despite this convenience, any order-preserving transformation of these numbers could also be used to index the states: for example, multiplying the original numbers by any positive constant (say, 2) preserves the ordering with a new set of indices, [2, 4, 6, 8, 10, 12], as does using the set of their natural logarithms, [0, .69, 1.10, 1.39, 1.61, 1.79]. In any order-preserving scale, lower number still mean a higher rank. The [1, 2, 3, . . .] ranking is easier to read, and it is convenient to imply by "number one" that the team finished first, by "number two" that it finished second, and so on. However, the particular set of ordered numerical names to be used is arbitrary. Any order-preserving relabelling of these names conveys the same ordinal information.

Three Issues in the Analysis of Ordinal Variables

Issue 1: Tied Observations. In the baseball example, no two teams had the same won-lost record; consequently, no two teams were tied in the final standings. Two observations are *tied* on an ordinal variable if they are assigned to the same variable state. Whether in baseball or statistics, rules should be specified as to what should be done with ties.

To be generally useful in social science, measures must be able to deal appropriately with ties. Going back to the Aberbach and Rockman bureaucrat sample, we have only three categories of party affiliation and five of support for social services. As an example, we will consider a subsample of 31 bureaucrats from three social services agencies, HEW, HUD, and OEO. Since, for both variables, there are far more bureaucrats than categories, we are guaranteed to have ties. The way ties are to be handled merits attention later in the paper; it is an important question that cannot be avoided. For example, differences in the way ties are handled account for major distinctions among three of the most commonly used measures of ordinal association: Somers' d_{yx}, Kendall's τ_b^2, and Goodman and Kruskal's gamma.

Issue 2: Predicting Single Observations vs. Pairs of Observations. A much more basic issue in dealing with ordinal association is whether the analysis should focus directly on single observations or on comparisons within pairs of observations. To clarify the distinction, we need to address an analytical problem involving two variables.

The two variables describing bureaucrats–namely, party affiliation and support for social services–will serve to illustrate the general analysis of association for ordinal variables. To ask if two such variables are associated or related is not a fully operational question. Consequently, we will focus instead on whether (and in what way) one variable is useful in *predicting* the other.

Consider the cross-classification shown as Table 1. Suppose the investigator used each bureaucrat's party affiliation (*Dem, Ind, Rep*) to predict the bureaucrat's support for increased social services (*left, left-center, center, right-center, right*). Let the statement x $\leadsto$ y mean, "if x then predict y" or "x tends to be a sufficient condition for y." Then the prediction $\mathcal{P}$, "*Dem* $\leadsto$ (*left* or *left-center*) & *Ind* $\leadsto$ *center* & *Rep* $\leadsto$ (*center* or *right-center* or *right*)," identifies the cells that are shaded in Table 1 as error events. Unshaded cells are successes for the prediction. Note that, for Democrats, two categories of the dependent variable constitute successes; for Republicans, three categories are successes.

Conventionally, predictions of this kind have not played much of a role in data analysis. The emphasis has been on predicting a single category of the dependent variable for each category of the independent variable. Such restrictions on the form of the predictions are not foreordained. Clearly, some scientific theories will vary in the precision with which they can predict outcomes and, alternatively, some categories of the independent variable may contain more information for prediction than others.

Predictions like $\mathcal{P}$ have three important advantages:

(1) Given any observation's state on the independent variable, we can make a definite prediction about its state on the dependent variable. If we are told that bureaucrat Nixman is a Republican, for example, we predict that he will be *center, right-center,* or *right* toward social services.

TABLE 1
Party Affiliation and Support for Social Services by Top-Level Bureaucrats in Social Service Agencies

Support for Increased Government Role in Social Services	Party Affiliation: Dem	Ind	Rep	
Left	12	3	1	16
Left-center	1	2	2	5
Center	0	3	4	7
Right-center	0	1	1	2
Right	0	0	1	1
	13	9	9	31 bureaucrats

Data Source: Aberbach and Rockman (1976, p. 460).

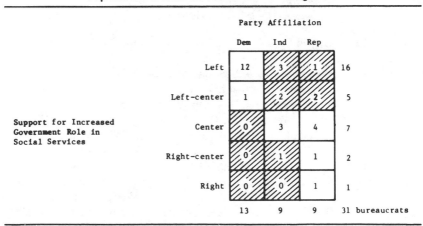

(2) A related advantage is that we can make a definite statement as to whether the prediction for each bureaucrat is correct or incorrect. If Mr. Nixman turned out to be *left* on social services, the prediction was wrong.

(3) Ties pose no problem for analyzing this kind of prediction.

In practice, ordinal variables have seldom been analyzed with such predictions. The social science literature frequently contains statements of the form, "Social services support tends to increase with a more liberal party affiliation," or, "There is a 'U-shaped' relation between support for social services and party affiliation." Also frequent are statements of the form, "The more liberal the party affiliation (X), the greater will be support for social services (Y)." Later in this paper we will make such statements operational and discuss ways of evaluating them. First, though, we need to evaluate propositions like $\mathcal{P}$.

How can we assess the agreement of a given set of data with such predictions? An oversimplified way would be to count the number of errors. Consider the distribution of the 31 bureaucrats in Table 1 and the proposition $\mathcal{P}$ that identifies the cells shaded there as error events. Counting the total number of bureaucrats who are assigned to some error cell, we discover that out of the 31 bureaucrats, we made errors in nine cases (3+1+2+2+0+0+1+0+0). This raw number of errors is not really adequate to evaluate the prediction, but it is at least a start.

It is less obvious what can be done about assessing the "Y increases with X" or "the more the X, the more the Y" type of statement. One approach to evaluating this proposition would be to try to find a specific prediction of observations that is consistent with it. For example, the prediction $\mathcal{P}$ used above is one that appears consistent with "Y increases with X." On the other hand, an alternative prediction,

$\mathcal{P}'$: *Dem* $\rightsquigarrow$ *left* or *left-center*
Ind $\rightsquigarrow$ *center* or *right-center* or *right*
Rep $\rightsquigarrow$ *left* or *left-center*

identifies the "U-shaped" pattern of unshaded cells shown in Table 2. The prediction $\mathcal{P}'$ makes 11 errors—two more than $\mathcal{P}$.

This prediction approach to ordinal data has hardly been applied in any of the social sciences. The approach that has been widely applied involves analyzing "The more the X, the more the Y" form in terms of predictions about *relative comparisons* of *pairs* of observations. Consider bureaucrats Amy and Nixman. Amy can be *more* liberal (in terms of party affiliation). This would happen if she were a *Democrat,* and he was an *Independent* or *Republican,* or if she were an *Independent* and he was a *Republican*. Alternatively, Amy and Nixman would have the *same* liberalism (tied) if both were *Dem,* if both were *Ind* or if both were *Rep*. Otherwise, Amy would be *less* liberal than *Nixman*. These three categories—*more, same, less*—are the only ones we can have that use only ordinal information in making comparisons. For this reason, we define these categories as the *condensed ordinal form of* X [2] derived from the original variable X (support

TABLE 2
An Alternative Prediction About Support for Social Services

Support for Increased Government Role in Social Services	Party Affiliation: Dem	Ind	Rep	
Left	12	3	1	16
Left-center	1	2	2	5
Center	0	3	4	7
Right-center	0	1	1	2
Right	0	0	1	1
	13	9	9	31 bureaucrats

Data Source: Aberbach and Rockman (1976, p. 460).

for party affiliation). The superscript on X^{*2} indicates that observation *pairs* are being compared on the variable X. We can also develop a condensed ordinal form for the social services variable.

With these new forms of the variables, we can now make predictions for pairs similar to the ones we originally made for observations. For example, consider the prediction, $\mathcal{P}^*$:

> If the first of two bureaucrats has a *more* liberal party affiliation than the second, his support for social services will be the *same* or *more* than that of the second bureaucrat. If the two bureaucrats are the *same* on liberalism, then they tend to give the *same* support to social services. If the first of the two bureaucrats is *less* liberal than the second, his support for social services will be the *same* or *less* than that of the second bureaucrat.

As a shorthand, we write

$$\mathcal{P}^*: \quad \textit{more} \rightsquigarrow \textit{more} \text{ or } \textit{same}, \quad \textit{same} \rightsquigarrow \textit{same}, \ \& \quad \textit{less} \rightsquigarrow \textit{same} \text{ or } \textit{less}$$

If we want to evaluate this prediction, we can make a table for the two condensed form variables similar to Table 1. If the 31 officials are Amy, Bob, Cal, . . . and Nixman, we note that they can be paired $31^2 = 961$ different ways as (Amy,Amy), (Amy,Bob), (Amy,Cal), . . . , (Amy,Nixman), (Bob,Amy), (Bob,Bob), (Bob,Cal), . . . , (Nixman,Nixman). Note that in 31 of these pairs [(Amy,Amy), (Bob,Bob), (Cal,Cal), . . . , (Nixman,Nixman)] the same bureaucrat appears twice. Table 3 locates each of the 961 pairs in the cross-classification

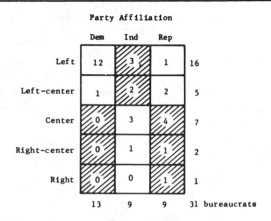

TABLE 3
A Prediction for Pairs

		Condensed Ordinal Form of Party Affiliation (Liberalism)			
		more	same	less	
Condensed Ordinal Form of Increased Social Services Support	more	221	70	22	313
	same	72	191	72	335
	less	22	70	221	313
		315	331	315	961 pairs of bureaucrats

of the *condensed form* variables. How Table 3 relates to Table 1 is deferred to section 3. For the moment, we note that, as in Table 1, we can look at the shaded cells in Table 3 that represent errors for $\mathcal{P}^*$ and count the number of incorrect pairs. There are 22 + 70 + 70 + 22 = 184 of the 961 pairs that are errors for $\mathcal{P}^*$.

Most widely used measures of ordinal association, such as gamma and various d and tau measures, can be related to this cross-tabulation of condensed form variables. These measures can be interpreted as being based on predictions that are operational statements of "the more the X, the more the Y," or, alternatively, "Y increases with X." The condensed form thus plays a central role in this essay.

Some writers have gone so far as to argue that the condensed form analysis of paired comparisons should be at least the predominant (if not the only) mode of analysis for ordinal variables:

> The restriction to pairs in the case of ordinal statistics is compatible with the inherently comparative nature of ordinal data. And in a fundamental sense, the empirical foundation of science is comparison and contrast rather than the study of a single, isolated observation, *in vacuo* [Somers, 1974: 231].

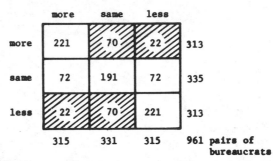

While we agree that comparison is a vital part of the scientific process, it can occur as part of the evaluation of the prediction and need not necessarily enter in defining the variables that are the subject of prediction. More importantly, for many purposes it may be more relevant to make predictions about single observations than about pairs. Certainly, some, perhaps most, researchers will attach greater interest to predicting the degree of support each bureaucrat actually gives to social services increases than to predicting how his support will compare to that of another bureaucrat.

The proponents of the condensed form (Table 3) may still respond that predictions such as $\mathcal{P}$ and $\mathcal{P}'$ (Tables 1 and 2) are not really ordinal but nominal. After all, even with simple nominal categories one could state predictions that would lead to patterns of shaded error cells as in the first two tables. In contrast, since the relations *more* and *less* are meaningless to simple categorization (Caucasian is neither *more* nor *less* than Native American), the condensed ordinal form requires at least ordinal measurement. With pairs, the ordinality thus affects the prediction via the manner in which the condensed form categories are defined.

Predictions for single observations can, however, also reflect the ordinal characteristic of the variables. The researcher will use the ordinality to impose some constraints as to the configuration, pattern or "shape" of the unshaded success cells. The proposition of Table 1 predicts a "monotone increasing" shape; Table 2 a "U-shape." Except in very unusual circumstances, there should be a single bloc of shaded cells or of unshaded cells in a given column or row. A prediction like that shown in Table 4 leads to a configuration of cells that seems unlikely to arise from a theory relating two *ordinal* variables. Thus, when variables are ordinal, the ordinality will influence the prediction, even for single observations.

Issue 3: Ordinal vs. Quantitative Variables. A final issue concerning ordinal variables asks whether they are worth much attention. Rather than devoting effort to improving methodologies for analyzing ordinal variables, Wilson (1970) and Blalock (1960) among others have argued that social scientists

TABLE 4
An Implausible Prediction for Two Ordinal Variables

		Party Affiliation			
		Dem	Ind	Rep	
Support for Increased Government Role in Social Services	Left	12	3	1	16
	Left-center	1	2	2	5
	Center	0	3	4	7
	Right-center	0	1	1	2
	Right	0	0	1	1
		13	9	9	31 bureaucrats

Data Source: Aberbach and Rockman (1976, p. 460).

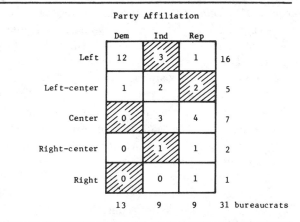

should seek to quantify concepts they now treat ordinally. After all, much of the advance in physical science might be attributed to quantification.

There are at least two related reasons which suggest that ordinal variables will long remain at the core of social science. First, ordinality appears to be important in many social phenomena. The ranking of people (in terms of their performance or seniority, for example) is often the primary criterion used to allocate rewards such as raises in pay and promotion to positions of higher responsibility, whether in professional baseball, Congress, business firms, or other institutions. Second, recent research in human cognition (Newell and Simon, 1972) suggests that it is useful to assume that people have limited information processing, hence quantifying, capacity. Similarly, in a different research tradition, mathematical economists and game theorists have actively sought to base social theory on ordinal rather than quantitative measures of preference. For example, it is plausible that, in response to a survey item, a voter can say that she preferred Reagan to Ford to Carter as president in 1976. Can she also provide a meaningful indication of *how much* she preferred Reagan to Ford relative to how much she preferred Ford to Carter? Viewed from the perspective of social choice theory or game theory, such a quantitative evaluation is equivalent to the voter's specifying the odds for a lottery between Reagan and Carter that would make her indifferent between the lottery and, on the other hand, a sure victory for Ford. While some psychophysicists would be prepared to argue that such quantitative judgments can be made, placing such a demand on a respondent in practice is both difficult and costly. Since typical measurements of political preferences are likely to remain ordinal, we need methods for analyzing ordinal variables.

Or do we? Some authors treat ordinal variables as quantitative by assigning numerical values to the variable states and then using Pearson r correlations in regression analysis methods designed for quantitative data (regression analysis is surveyed in Uslaner, forthcoming). For example, the *left, left-center, center, right-center,* and *right* ordinal categories could be assigned values 1, 2, 3, 4, and 5. Does this arbitrary numerical assignment eventually lead us to different substantive conclusions? Consider the data in Table 1. Pearson's r^2, the standard measure of association for quantitative data, equals .456 when these numerical values are used. In many respects, as we show later, Kendall's τ_b^2 is an ordinal variable analog of r^2. Its value for the table is .402, .05 less than r^2. Both measures can lie between 0 (no association) and 1 ("perfect" association). For other data sets, the difference between r^2 and τ_b^2 can easily be greater or less than .05. Whether such differences are substantively important depends on the purposes of a specific investigation but, clearly, the differences will sometimes matter.

Focusing on differences between r^2 and some ordinal measure such as τ_b^2 which evaluates "the more of this, the more of that" really misses the central point. Neither the "linear" pattern of association examined via r^2 nor "the more of this, the more of that" may be the correct expression of the investigator's research hypothesis. We show later that different measures of "association" can give widely different values when applied to the same data. It is appropriate, therefore, to proceed to a serious analysis of the measurement of association between ordinal variables. We prefer to recast this problem as one of evaluating the prediction success of a specific proposition. Section 2 discusses the evaluation of bivariate prediction success for single observations and develops the quadrant measure and Cohen's kappa as special measures for particular propositions. Section 3 discusses the evaluation of prediction success for propositions about pairs of observations, developing measures proposed by Goodman and Kruskal, Kendall, Kim, Somers, and Wilson as special cases. We also interpret Spearman's rho_S as a measure for the prediction of observation triples. In section 4, we illustrate how an ordinal variable may be analyzed in conjunction with a nominal variable or a quantitative variable. Section 5 discusses the multivariate analysis of ordinal variables, and section 6 briefly surveys questions of computation and statistical inference.

2. BIVARIATE PREDICTION FOR SINGLE OBSERVATIONS

Population versus Sample

Let us go back to our bureaucrats and attempt to evaluate the original prediction represented in Table 1:

$\mathcal{P}$: *Dem* $\rightsquigarrow$ *left* or *left-center*
Ind $\rightsquigarrow$ *center*
Rep $\rightsquigarrow$ *center, right-center,* or *right*

To evaluate this prediction, we must first ask how the data were obtained or are to be interpreted. In this case the data are the results of a sample survey. Obviously, there are problems in generalizing from the survey results to a relevant population. For now, we nonetheless consider the 31 bureaucrats as a population. The fundamental question in the evaluation of predictions is most simply stated in terms of a population: what is the appropriate measure? The problems that arise when we try to estimate the true population value of a measure from sample data can be deferred and mentioned briefly later.

To evaluate the prediction, we calculate its proportionate reduction in error. The (hoped-for) reduction occurs when we make a prediction for each case with knowledge of its independent variable state in contrast to predicting without such information. That is, we wish to compare the observed error rate when a prediction $\mathcal{P}$ is applied to a given population with the error rate for a benchmark prediction that does not make use of the independent variable information.

Predicting With Knowledge of the Independent Variable State

It is easy to use the proposition, $\mathcal{P}$, to make a prediction for each bureaucrat knowing his party affiliation. We are given each of the 31 officials, one at a time. For each bureaucrat, knowing whether he is *Dem, Ind,* or *Rep,* we make the appropriate prediction associated with $\mathcal{P}$. If the prediction is wrong, we add one to our error total. Thus, for the 13 Democrats, we predict *left* or *left-center* and consequently make no errors (see Table 1). The proposition $\mathcal{P}$ predicts *center* for each of the nine Independents so the six non-*center* cases are errors. Finally, the prediction for Republicans identifies *left* and *left-center* as error events, contributing three errors for the nine Republican bureaucrats. Therefore, we observe nine (0+6+3) prediction errors, the number of bureaucrats who lie in the set of cells that are shaded in Table 1.

The number nine, or even the fraction 9/31, is not enough information to evaluate the prediction adequately. For example, what if all 31 bureaucrats were Democrats and we still made nine errors, as shown in Table 5? Clearly we are not gaining much from knowing the party affiliation state here. Or, put differently, we cannot say that the two variables are "associated" when one of the variables does not vary. Similarly, consider Table 6 which shows a hypothetical population and the error cells of a prediction. The prediction there also makes nine errors, but we would want to regard them as more serious than those in Table 1. After all, the prediction of Table 6 makes the wrong prediction for every bureaucrat (Independent) for whom it possibly *could* be wrong. The total of nine errors, then, will only be meaningful if it is compared to an appropriate benchmark.

TABLE 5
Hypothetical Population Without Variation in Party Affiliation

Support for Increased Government Role in Social Services		Party Affiliation: Dem	Ind	Rep	
	Left	22	0	0	22
	Left-center	0	0	0	0
	Center	3	0	0	3
	Right-center	3	0	0	3
	Right	3	0	0	3
		31	0	0	31 bureaucrats

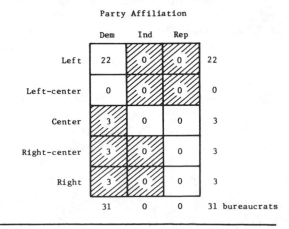

TABLE 6

Hypothetical Population for Which Prediction Shown is Always Wrong

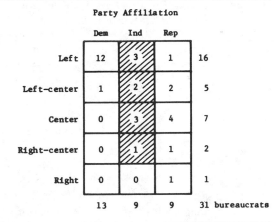

Support for Increased Government Role in Social Services	Party Affiliation: Dem	Ind	Rep	
Left	12	3	1	16
Left-center	1	2	2	5
Center	0	3	4	7
Right-center	0	1	1	2
Right	0	0	1	1
	13	9	9	31 bureaucrats

Predicting Without Information About the Independent Variable State

As a benchmark, we replicate the prediction of $\wp$, but without knowledge of the actual independent variable state. The motivation of this procedure is beyond the scope of this paper. (For details, see Hildebrand, Laing, and Rosenthal, 1974a; 1977, ch. 3.) Suffice it to say that the benchmark prediction is both (a) *a priori* in the sense that no information about the predicted (dependent) variable is used, and (b) invariant with changes in category definition and ordering that have no effect on the prediction being evaluated. (As an example of definitional changes, consider combining the categories *left* and *left-center* into a single category *any left*. Also combine *right-center* and *right* into *any right*. The prediction *Dem* $\rightsquigarrow$ *any left, Ind* $\rightsquigarrow$ *center,* and *Rep* $\rightsquigarrow$ (*center* or *any right*) is logically equivalent to $\wp$.) Moreover (c) the benchmark procedure is comparable to that used when each observation's state of the independent variable is known since the same number of each type of prediction is made in the two information conditions. Thus, the same predictions are made in the benchmark procedure, but this time they are made without each observation's independent variable state. It turns out, as we shall see, that most of the existing measures of ordinal association can be given a unified interpretation via this benchmark.

The replication procedure, as applied to the data in Table 1, follows. Thirteen of the 31 bureaucrats are selected at random. For each of these we predict *left* or *left-center,* the same prediction we made earlier for Democrats. Error occurs if the case is *center, right center,* or *right*. Similarly, we predict *center* for nine cases drawn at random, thus replicating the predictions made earlier for Independents. Any of these nine bureaucrats who is not described as *center* on the support variable is an error. Finally, again drawing nine bureaucrats at random and without knowing their party, we predict *center, right-center,* or *right,* replicating the predictions made earlier for each of the Republicans. Any bureaucrat who is *left* or *left-center* represents an error for this prediction. Note that in the benchmark procedure, we need to know the marginal totals for the independent variable, but do not know each individual case's state on the variable. Moreover, we need no information about the population's distribution (marginal or otherwise) on the dependent variable in order to *make* the prediction.

We obviously always need dependent variable information to calculate the extent to which the predictions were wrong. To begin this calculation we note that in the whole population there are 7 + 2 + 1 = 10 bureaucrats whose support for social welfare is *center, right-center,* or *right,* the error events for the benchmark replications of the Democratic predictions. Since we are drawing at random from the whole population, an error therefore will occur with probability 10/31, or, on average, in a little less than one out of three predictions. Since there are 13 such replication predictions, we expect, *on average,* to make 13(10/31) = 4.19 errors.

For the replication of the predictions made earlier for Independents, only *center* is not an error event. In the whole population there are 31 – 7 = 24 cases that are not *center.* The error probability for the *center* prediction is thus 24/31. Multiplying by the nine cases for which this prediction was made leads to 9(24/31) = 6.97 expected errors. Finally, for the benchmark replication of the predictions made earlier for Republicans, the probability of error is 21/31 since there are 16 *left* and 5 *left-center* bureaucrats in the entire population of 31 bureaucrats. Therefore, this portion of the replication is expected to make 9(21/31) = 6.10 errors. Summing over all the predictions, there are $\frac{1}{31}$ [13(10) + 9(24) + 9(21)] = 535/31 = 17.26 errors expected from this replication.

The $\nabla_{\mathcal{P}}$ Measure

Define the measure of prediction success as

$$\nabla_{\mathcal{P}} = \frac{\text{Expected Errors} - \text{Observed Errors}}{\text{Expected Errors}}$$

$$= 1 - (\text{Observed Errors}/\text{Expected Errors})$$

$$= 1 - 9/17.26 = .479$$

If there had been no observed error, the measure would have been equal to 1.0. If there had been as many observed errors as expected in this replication, the measure would have been zero. In fact, the prediction led to a little less than 50 percent error reduction.

If the prediction had been that illustrated in Table 6, the reader can calculate that

$$\text{Observed errors} = 3 + 2 + 3 + 1 = 9$$

$$\text{Expected errors} = 9\ [(16 + 5 + 7 + 2)/31] = 270/31 = 8.71$$

$$\nabla = 1 - 9/8.71 \ = - .033$$

(The subscript $\mathcal{P}$ on ∇ emphasizes that the $\nabla_{\mathcal{P}}$ measure always reflects a specific prediction. When the prediction being applied is evident, as in the preceding example, we may omit the subscript.) Not only does this value accord with our earlier assessment that the prediction should be less successful for Table 6 than for Table 1, but it also shows that the $\nabla_{\mathcal{P}}$ measure of prediction success can be negative. This occurs when, as in this case, the prediction does worse than the benchmark replication.

To generalize this measure beyond the bureaucrats example requires some notation. The general table has R rows and C columns. In the example of Table 1, R = 5 and C = 3. The letter i indexes the row, i = 1,2, . . . , R and j = 1,2, . . . , C the columns. In the example i = 3 designates the *center* row. Rather than speaking in terms of number of cases, it is more convenient to speak in terms of probabilities. In a finite population, the probability P_{ij} of an observation having both row state i and column state j is the number of cases in the corresponding cell in the population divided by the population size. In the example, $P_{22} = 2/31$, $P_{43} = 1/31$, and so on. Now consider the row and column totals ("marginals"). The marginal probability of row i is designated as $P_{i.}$, of column j as $P_{.j}$. Once again, we can divide numbers of cases by total population size, so for the rows of Table 1,

$$P_{1.} = 16/31, \quad P_{2.} = 5/31, \quad P_{3.} = 7/31, \quad P_{4.} = 2/31, \quad P_{5.} = 1/31$$

while for the columns,

$$P_{.1} = 13/31, \quad P_{.2} = P_{.3} = 9/13$$

Overall, the following identities must hold. First summing over columns gives the row total

$$\sum_{j=1}^{C} P_{ij} = P_{i.}$$

and summing over rows yields

$$\sum_{i=1}^{R} P_{ij} = P_{.j}$$

Finally,

$$\sum_{i=1}^{R}\sum_{j=1}^{C} P_{ij} = \sum_{i=1}^{R} P_{i.} = \sum_{j=1}^{C} P_{.j} = 1.0$$

Each cell (ij) in the table can be assigned an error measure, ω_{ij}. If the prediction for the table identifies the cell as a success, then $\omega_{ij} = 0$. Often, an investigator will want to treat all errors equally. That is, all observations that fall into error cells are assigned the same "degree" or "amount" of error. Without loss of generality, it is then appropriate to set $\omega_{ij} = 1$ for every cell (ij) that is an error cell. If the investigator wishes to assign different degrees of severity to various error events, he can assign any error weight strictly greater than zero to an error cell. For example, such differential weighting of errors will be shown to underly several measures of ordinal association, reflecting the idea that ties might be regarded as less serious errors than are outright reversals of order. Again without loss of generality, it often is convenient to set the largest such error weight equal to one. In the bureaucrats example of Table 1, we implicitly assigned all error events equal weight: so $\omega_{12} = \omega_{13} = \omega_{22} = \omega_{23} = \omega_{31} = \omega_{41} = \omega_{42} = \omega_{51} = \omega_{52} = 1$, and every other $\omega_{ij} = 0$.

Given the ω_{ij} notation to represent a bivariate prediction $\mathcal{P}$ and the P_{ij} notation for the general specification of population probabilities, the procedure we have illustrated for calculating observed and expected error rates and then forming the proportionate-reduction-in-error measure leads to the general definition:

$$\nabla_{\mathcal{P}} = 1 - (\text{Observed Errors/Expected Errors})$$

$$= 1 - \frac{\sum_{i=1}^{R}\sum_{j=1}^{C} \omega_{ij} P_{ij}}{\sum_{i=1}^{R}\sum_{j=1}^{C} \omega_{ij} P_{i.} P_{.j}}$$

For the prediction and data shown in Table 1,

Observed Error Rate = 0 + 3/31 + 1/31 + 0 + 2/31 + 2/31 + 0 + 0 + 0 + 0 + 1/31 + 0 + 0 + 0 + 0 = 9/31 = .290

Expected Error Rate = 0 + (16/31) (9/31) + (16/31) (9/31) + 0 + (5/31) (9/31) + (5/31) (9/31) + (7/31) (13/31) + 0 + 0 + (2/31) (13/31) + (2/31) (9/31) + 0 + (1/31) (13/31) + (1/31) (9/31) + 0 = 535/961 = .557

$\nabla_{\mathcal{P}} = 1 - .290/.557 = .479$

Similar but slightly abbreviated calculations for the data and proposition of Table 4 show

Observed Error Rate = 3/31 + 2/31 + 0/31 + 1/31 + 0/31 = 6/31 = .194

Expected Error Rate = (16/31) (9/31) + (5/31) (9/31) + (7/31) (13/31) + (2/31) (9/31) + (1/31) (13/31) = 311/961 = .324

$\nabla_{\mathcal{P}} = 1 - .194/.324 = .402$

Precision. From the computation of the ∇ measures for Table 1 and Table 4, one can note that the "expected" error rate for Table 4, 311/961 = .324, is less than that for Table 1, 535/961 = .557. In fact, there must be fewer expected errors in Table 4 because every error cell in Table 4 is also an error cell in Table 1 and Table 1 also has some additional error cells. An event that is an error for Table 4 is always an error for Table 1, but the converse is not true, implying that Table 1 represents a "tougher" or more precise prediction. In general, the "expected" error rate measures the *precision* of a prediction. We denote this rate by the symbol U.

Dominance. We say that one prediction *dominates* another when the prediction has a higher ∇ (prediction success) value and at least as great a U (prediction precision) value than the other or, alternatively, a higher U value and at least as great a ∇ value. For example, we have seen that the prediction represented in Table 1 has both a higher ∇ value and a higher U value than the prediction represented in Table 4. Consequently, the first prediction cominates the second.

Statistical Independence and ∇. Inspection of the expressions for ∇ show that ∇ = 0 whenever the "observed" errors equal the "expected," that is, when

$$\sum_i \sum_j \omega_{ij} P_{ij} = \sum_i \sum_j \omega_{ij} P_{i.} P_{.j}$$

To see when this condition is met, consider another "population," the U.S. Senate, which conveniently has exactly 100 members. Assume that we had developed two scales for the senators (like those for the bureaucrats), based this time on roll call votes rather than interview responses. What if the data were as below?

		Scale X			
		high	med	low	
Scale Y	hot	3	6	1	10
	warm	6	12	2	20
	cool	12	24	4	40
	cold	9	18	3	30
		30	60	10	100 senators

Note that the entries in any column in this table are proportional to those in any other column. A similar statement holds for the row entries. Consider first the 30 senators who are "high" on scale X and, therefore, lie in the first column of the table. The proportion of these "high" senators in each of the scale Y categores are, respectively,

$$3/30, 6/30, 12/30, \text{and } 9/30$$

or, equivalently,

$$.1, .2, .4, \text{and } .3$$

These same proportions hold for senators in the "medium" and "low" columns as well. From this it follows that these same proportions apply to the set of all 100 senators so that the row marginals also equal

$$.1, .2, .4, \text{and } .3$$

In other words, for every column state x_j and row category y_i,

$$P(y_i \,|\, x_j) = P_{ij}/P_{.j} = P_{i.}$$

For example,

$$P(y_3 \,|\, x_2) = 24/60 = .40 = P_{3.}$$

Since this .40 figure is the probability of y_3 whatever the state x_j, knowing the independent variable state of an observation does *not* provide any information as to the likelihood that y_3 will occur or, in fact, that any other state y_i will occur. (As an exercise, show that a similar results holds if Y is the independent variable, X dependent.) Consequently, knowledge of the X state cannot benefit any prediction about Y. This implies that all ∇ values for such a distribution, whatever the specification of the error cells and weights, ought to be zero. From $P_{ij}/P_{.j} = P_{i.}$ for this special case, it follows that every $P_{ij} = P_{i.}P_{.j}$ and "observed" errors equal "expected" errors, hence $\nabla = 0$.

When $P_{ij} = P_{i.}P_{.j}$ holds for all i and j, the variables are said to be *statistically independent*. The "expected" error rate then equals the rate that would occur in a population that exhibited statistical independence and had marginal probabilities identical to those of the population under analysis. We ought to point out that ∇ can also equal zero when the variables are *not* statistically independent. All that is required is that the *sum* of probabilities (weighted by ω_{ij}) in the error cells equals the *sum* that would occur under statistical independence. This directly parallels the situation for quantitative variables where statistical independence is a sufficient *but not necessary* condition for a zero correlation.

The Quadrant Measure: A Special Application for Ordinal Variables

A particular application of the general ∇ model is the quadrant measure discussed by Kruskal (1958). To illustrate, assume we were dealing with a hypothetical population of 10 bureaucrats that is cross-classified in Table 7(a). Note that half the bureaucrats are Republicans and the other half are either *Ind* or *Dem*. Similarly, (*left* and *left-center*) vs. (*center, center-right,* and *right*) give us a "50-50" split (in this case, 5-5) on social services. Heavy black lines divide the table into four quadrants. Consider the prediction identifying the shaded cells in Table 7(a) as error events. This proposition can be written equivalently as x (*Dem* or *Ind*) predicts y (*left* or *left-center*) and $\bar{x}$ (*Rep*) predicts $\bar{y}$ (*center* or *right-center* or *right*). For short, we write $(x \rightsquigarrow y)$ & $(\bar{x} \rightsquigarrow \bar{y})$, or in even more compact notation, $x \leftrightsquigarrow y$, analogous to the formal logic expression "x if and only if y." In other words, this proposition predicts that the data should tend to be concentrated in the xy and $\bar{x}\bar{y}$ quadrants; the $x\bar{y}$ and $\bar{x}y$ quadrants are the error events. In Table 7(b), note that there are six observed errors. Whether we predict y or $\bar{y}$, without knowledge of party affiliation, we will err in one-half of the predictions, or five cases on average, because the 50-50 split makes y and $\bar{y}$ equally likely. In particular, we will expect to make five errors in applying the replication procedure. In this case, the

$$\text{quadrant measure} = 1 - (\text{Observed Errors})/(\text{Expected Errors})$$
$$= 1 - 6/5 = -.200$$

In general,

$$\text{quadrant measure} = 1 - \frac{P_{y\bar{x}} + P_{\bar{y}x}}{P_{y.}P_{.\bar{x}} + P_{\bar{y}.}P_{.x}}$$

$$= 1 - \frac{P_{y\bar{x}} + P_{\bar{y}x}}{(1/2)(1/2) + (1/2)(1/2)}$$

$$= 1 - 2(P_{y\bar{x}} + P_{\bar{y}x})$$

$$= 1 - 4P_{y\bar{x}}$$

where x is a combined category that contains the half of the observations that are in the "highest" categories on the independent variable and $\bar{x}$ combines the "lowest" categories. The states y and $\bar{y}$ are defined similarly for the dependent variable.[1]

As to its advantages, the quadrant measure does predict single observations and is easy to compute. Unlike some of the standard measures for pairs, however, it cannot be interpreted as being based upon a totally a priori prediction

TABLE 7
The Quadrant Prediction in a Hypothetical Population of Ten Bureaucrats

(a) The original table:

Support for Increased Social Services (rows) by Party Affiliation (Liberalism) (columns)

	Dem	Ind	Rep	
Left	1	0	1	2
Left-center	1	0	2	3
Center	0	3	0	3
Right-center	0	0	1	1
Right	0	0	1	1
	2	3	5	10 bureaucrats

(b) The logically equivalent representation in a 2 x 2 table:

Support for Increased Social Services (rows)

	x (Dem or Ind)	$\bar{x}$ (Rep)	
y (Left or Left-center)	2	3	5
$\bar{y}$ (Right, Right-center, or Center)	3	2	5
	5	5	10 bureaucrats

since we must have information as to where (if anywhere) the 50-50 (median) split occurs on the dependent variable. A more important weakness of the measure is that the 50-50 split needed to apply the measure will occur only rarely in practice and in fact is guaranteed not to occur in a finite population with an odd number of total observations. (The quadrant measure, in fact, is most readily thought of as being applied to an infinite population where all observations are strongly ordered—no ties—on both variables.)

Modification for Uneven Splits: When an exact 50-50 split fails to exist, there will be one category that straddles a 50-50 division of the observations. If this happens for variable X, let us relabel this category as x'_2. Those categories higher than the straddling category can be relabelled x'_1, those lower, x'_3. A similar definition is made for Y.

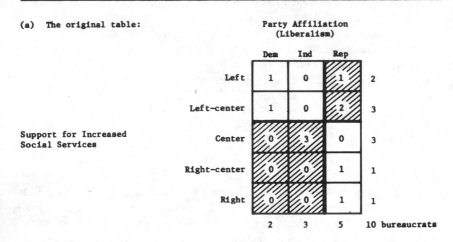

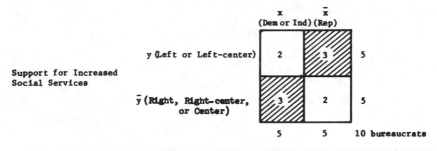

Now let the modified quadrant prediction be:

$$x_1' \rightsquigarrow (y_1' \text{ or } y_2')$$

$$x_2' \rightsquigarrow (y_1', y_2', \text{or } y_3')$$

$$x_3' \rightsquigarrow (y_2' \text{ or } y_3')$$

If there is an exact 50-50 split on both variables, then the middle categories (x_2' and y_2') are empty and the prediction becomes that of the quadrant measure. It is quite possible that one of the redefined categories can be empty. For example, in Table 1, over half the population is *left* on social services, implying that *left* is y_2' and that y_1' is empty. While ∇ could be computed for the modified quadrant prediction even if y_1' is empty, for illustrative purposes it is more instructive to consider the modification for the population of bureaucrats in non-social services agencies. As shown in Table 8, x_1' is *Dem*, x_2' is *Ind*, and x_3' is *Rep* while y_1' is *left* or *left-center*, y_2' is *center*, and y_3' is *right* or *right-center*.

Applying the general definition of ∇ to the modified quadrant prediction, as indicated by the error cells shown in Table 8, we obtain

$$\text{"modified quadrant measure"} = 1 - \frac{P_{1'3'} + P_{3'1'}}{P_{1'.}P_{.3'} + P_{3'.}P_{.1'}}$$

For Table 8 this measure equals

$$1 - \frac{(6/75) + (4/75)}{(28/75)(24/75) + (25/75)(35/75)} = 1 - \frac{.133}{.275} = .515$$

The major weakness of the quadrant measure, even if modified to allow for uneven splits, is that it evaluates a single, fixed prediction. This prediction underlying the measure may have little to do with a particular research hypothesis stated by an investigator a priori (prior to data analysis). Similarly, in ex post data analysis, the quadrant measure may miss an important relation in the data. For example, although the quadrant measure was negative for Table 7, applying the original proposition $\mathcal{P}$, developed for Table 1, to the Table 7 data shows that $\nabla_{\mathcal{P}} = .464$ and $U = .560$. Thus, the original proposition achieves substantially better prediction success with an accompanying increase in precision. By shifting predictions, we have caused the number for Table 7 to jump from −.200 to +.464, showing how important it is for the statistical measure to be attuned to the investigator's specific research hypothesis.

A related weakness of the quadrant measure is that it can have the same value in quite different populations. By inspection, Table 9 can be seen not to support the "Y increases with X" type of statement since six cases occur

TABLE 8

Party Affiliation and Support for Social Services Among Top-Level Bureaucrats in Non-Social Service Agencies

(a) The original data:

Support for Increased Government Role in Social Services (rows) by Party Affiliation (columns)

	Dem	Ind	Rep	
Left	6	3	2	11
Left-center	11	2	4	17
Center	14	4	4	22
Right-center	2	4	8	14
Right	2	3	6	11
	35	16	24	75 bureaucrats

(b) A coarser representation:

Party Affiliation

	Dem x'_1	Ind x'_2	Rep x'_3	
Left or Left-center y'_1	17	5	6	28
Center y'_2	14	4	4	22
Right or Right-center y'_3	4	7	14	25
	35	16	24	75 bureaucrats

Note: Vertically shaded cells are errors for **modified** quadrant measure. Horizontally shaded cells are errors for kappa.

Data Source: Aberbach and Rockman (1976, p. 460).

in the extreme cells at the lower left and upper right corners of the table. Likewise, applying the original proposition $\mathcal{P}$ to this table shows $\nabla_{\mathcal{P}} = -.296$. In contrast, we saw that Table 7 shows $\mathcal{P}$ to be moderately successful with $\nabla_{\mathcal{P}} = +.464$. Yet, for both tables, the quadrant measure is $-.200$.

Cohen's Kappa: Another Application

When both variables have the same number of categories (R = C), a prominent prediction is, for all i = 1, . . . , R, $\kappa: x_i \rightsquigarrow y_i$. That is, predict the data

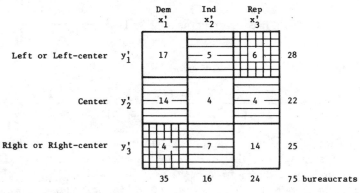

TABLE 9
An Alternative Table for Application of the Quadrant Measure

Support for Increased Government Role in Social Services		Party Affiliation: Dem	Ind	Rep	
	Left	0	1	3	4
	Left-center	1	0	0	1
	Center	0	0	1	1
	Right-center	0	0	1	1
	Right	3	0	0	3
		4	1	5	10 bureaucrats

Note: Vertical shading shows error cells for quadrant measure. Horizontal shading shows error cells for the proposition $\wp$ as in Table 1.

tend to fall on the main diagonal. For this prediction, we leave it to the reader as an exercise to show that the ∇ measure for unweighted errors simplifies to

$$\nabla_\kappa = \frac{\sum_i P_{ii} - \sum_i P_{i.} P_{.i}}{1 - \sum_i P_{i.} P_{.i}} = \text{kappa}$$

where kappa is a measure defined by Cohen (1960, 1968).

Like the quadrant measure, this prediction (κ) can be seen as an attempt to capture part of the "Y increases with X" statement. Note that if one variable has more categories than another, arbitrary combinations of various adjacent categories can always be used to make R = C. Which particular categories are combined will, of course, affect the value of kappa.

For the data in Table 8(b), we find

$$\sum_i P_{ii} = (17 + 4 + 14)/75 = 35/75 = .467$$

$$\sum_i P_{i.} P_{.i} = \left(\frac{28}{75}\right)\left(\frac{35}{75}\right) + \left(\frac{22}{75}\right)\left(\frac{16}{75}\right) + \left(\frac{25}{75}\right)\left(\frac{24}{75}\right) = 1932/5625 = .343$$

$$\text{kappa} = \frac{.467 - .343}{1 - .343} = .188$$

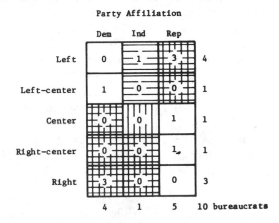

Note that the kappa prediction represented in Table 8 is logically equivalent to *Dem* $\rightsquigarrow$ (*left* or *left-center*), *Ind* $\rightsquigarrow$ *center*, and *Rep* $\rightsquigarrow$ (*Right-center* or *right*) for the original Table 8(a). One can check that these two equivalent propositions have identical ∇ values.

Suppose we transform Table 8(b) into a 2 x 2 table by combining y_2' and y_3' and combining *Ind* and *Rep*. Kappa for this table is based on the prediction *Dem* $\rightsquigarrow$ (*left* or *left-center*), *Ind* $\rightsquigarrow$ (*center, right-center* or *right*), and *Rep* $\rightsquigarrow$ (*center, right-center* or *right*). Kappa has a different value, namely .213, for the 2 x 2 table than it does for the original Table 8(b). This example illustrates a general point. When applying standard measures of association for ordinal variables, including those in the next section, changing from finer to coarser classifications or vice versa changes the underlying prediction represented in the measure (Goodman and Kruskal, 1954: 737-738). Consequently, the value of the measure also will be affected, often substantially.

Sensitivity Analysis for Predictions of Ordinal Variables: An Application to Reliability Assessment

Kappa was originally proposed by a psychologist, Jacob Cohen, as a measure of judgment reliability. Problems associated with the measurement of judgment reliability are prominent in various contexts of social science. The organization Freedom House (as reported in *Le Monde,* Jan. 4-5, 1976: 2) rated the 144 UN members as to whether they were *very free, free,* or *not free*. There were 16 *very free,* 23 *free,* and 105 *not free* countries. Another rater might give quite different ratings. Kappa gives a measure of the extent to which one rater's ranking predicts the other's (or vice versa, since $x_i \rightsquigarrow y_i$ for all i is logically equivalent to $y_j \rightsquigarrow x_j$ for all j). Cohen also proposed a weighted kappa (∇_κ with error weights) to allow for varying degrees of error severity. The weights can be especially useful with ordinal data.

Partial Order of Error Weights: How can we assign the weights to the UN ratings, where R=C=3? We know that an observation on the major diagonal is a success, so $\omega_{11} = \omega_{22} = \omega_{33} = 0$. Moreover, it would be reasonable to assume that when rater X says *very free* and rater Y says *not free,* the error is the same as when the reverse occurs. Put differently, observing *not free* when *very free* is predicted constitutes the same degree of error as observing *very free* when not *free* is predicted. (An analogous symmetry occurs in the use of squared error with quantitative variables.) Consequently, $\omega_{31} = \omega_{13}$. Also by symmetry, $\omega_{21} = \omega_{12}$ and $\omega_{32} = \omega_{23}$. (In the general case, $\omega_{ji} = \omega_{ij}$.) In the 3x3 example, therefore, we have only three unique non-zero weights: ω_{31}, ω_{21}, and ω_{32}.

What does the ordinal character of the variables tell us about their relative values? We can justify some relations among the error weights. Clearly, for any observations predicted to be *very free*, the outcome *not free* is at least as bad an error as is *free*, so $\omega_{31} \geqslant \omega_{21}$. Also, *not free* is no less serious an error when *very free* is predicted than when only *free* is predicted, so $\omega_{31} \geqslant \omega_{32}$. Thus, so far we have

$$\omega_{31} = \omega_{13} \geqslant \omega_{21} = \omega_{12} \geqslant 0$$

$$\omega_{31} = \omega_{13} \geqslant \omega_{32} = \omega_{23} \geqslant 0$$

$$\omega_{11} = \omega_{22} = \omega_{33} = 0$$

Without loss of generality, we can set the largest error weight equal to one, so $\omega_{31} = \omega_{13} = 1$. However, we may be unwilling to establish a relation between $\omega_{32} = \omega_{23}$ and $\omega_{21} = \omega_{12}$ because we cannot assess whether observing *free* when *very free* is predicted is more serious an error than when *not free* is predicted. Since we have established ordinal relations between some, but not all, of the error weights, we have only a partial order of the weights. This partial order is diagrammed in Figure 1.

Component Predictions: Now consider the three cross classifications in Table 10. Each of these tables contain two of the six error cells for the major diagonal (kappa) prediction shown in Table 11. Each of the three tables can be taken to represent components of the prediction

$$\kappa_i : x_i \rightsquigarrow y_i \quad \text{for all } i$$

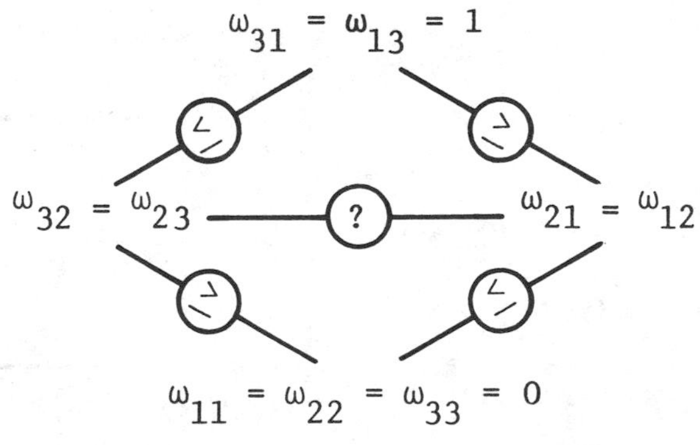

Figure 1: Partial Order of Error Weights for Kappa in a 3 x 3 Table

TABLE 10
The Three Components of κ for a 3 x 3 Table

(a) $\kappa^{(31)}$:

$x_1 \rightsquigarrow (y_1 \text{ or } y_2)$,

$x_2 \rightsquigarrow (y_1, y_2 \text{ or } y_3)$

& $x_3 \rightsquigarrow (y_2 \text{ or } y_3)$

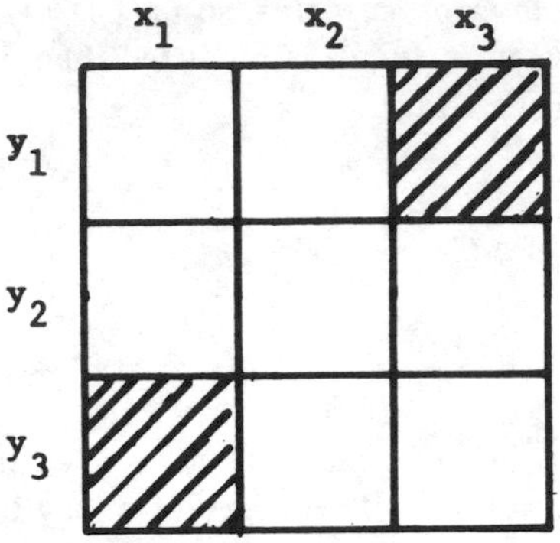

(b) $\kappa^{(21)}$:

$x_1 \rightsquigarrow (y_1 \text{ or } y_3)$,

$x_2 \rightsquigarrow (y_2 \text{ or } y_3)$

& $x_3 \rightsquigarrow (y_1, y_2 \text{ or } y_3)$

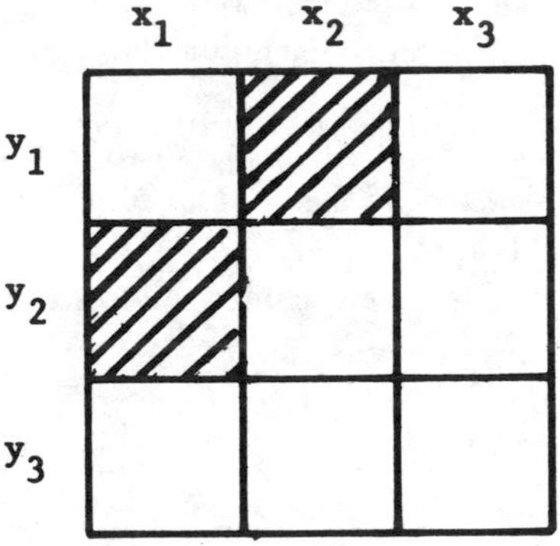

(c) $\kappa^{(32)}$:

$x_1 \rightsquigarrow (y_1, y_2 \text{ or } y_3)$,

$x_2 \rightsquigarrow (y_1 \text{ or } y_2)$

& $x_3 \rightsquigarrow (y_1 \text{ or } y_2)$

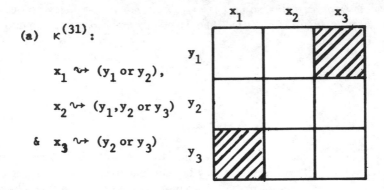

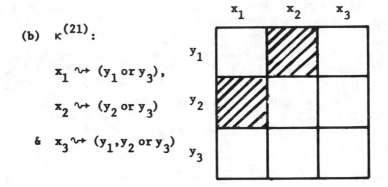

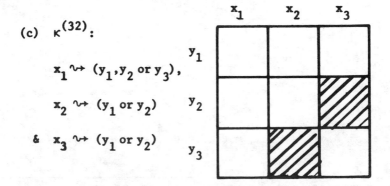

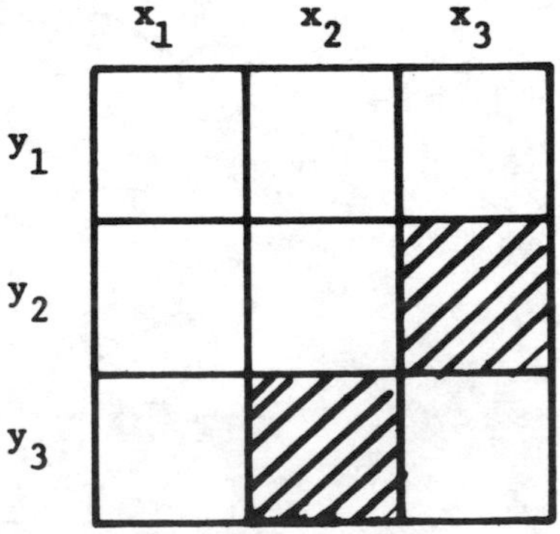

TABLE 11
Cross-Tabulation of Two Hypothetical Ratings of 144 UN Members

			Rater X			
			x_1	x_2	x_3	
			Very Free	Free	Not Free	
Rater Y	y_1	Very Free	14	1	1	16
	y_2	Free	3	3	17	23
	y_3	Not Free	1	14	90	105
			18	18	108	144 UN members

Shading shows error cells for K: $x_i \sim\!\!\rightarrow y_i$, $i = 1,2,3$.

The first component is named $\kappa^{(31)}$ since it corresponds to cells with error weight ω_{31}. It can be expressed as

$$\kappa^{(31)}: x_1 \sim\!\!\rightarrow (y_1 \text{ or } y_2) \; \&$$
$$x_2 \sim\!\!\rightarrow (y_1 \text{ or } y_2 \text{ or } y_3) \; \&$$
$$x_3 \sim\!\!\rightarrow (y_2 \text{ or } y_3)$$

Define $\kappa^{(21)}$ and $\kappa^{(32)}$ analogously.

∇ *as a Weighted Average of Component* ∇*'s:* It can be shown (again a possible exercise for the reader) that

$$\nabla_{\kappa,\omega} = \frac{1}{U^{(31)} + \omega_{21} U^{(21)} + \omega_{32} U^{(32)}} \, [U^{(31)}\nabla^{(31)} + \omega_{21} U^{(21)}\nabla^{(21)} + \omega_{32} U^{(32)}\nabla^{(32)}]$$

$$= \frac{1}{.174 + .034\,\omega_{21} + .211\,\omega_{32}} \, [(.174)(.920) + \omega_{21}(.034)(.179) + \omega_{32}(.211)(-.021)]$$

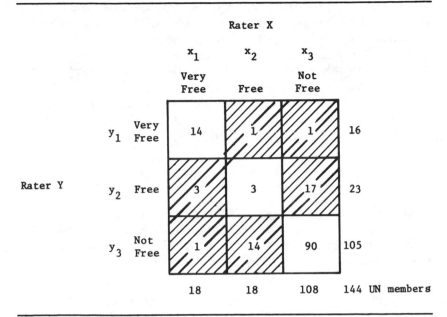

Specifically, $\nabla_{K,\omega}$ equals a weighted average of ∇'s for the three component predictions, the weights being the product of the error weights and the precision terms, U, for each component. We find the largest component is $\nabla^{(13)} = .920$ for the hypothetical data in Table 11. By our earlier analysis of the partial order of the weights, this component must be included with the largest possible weight (1.0). Since adding components with lower ∇'s into the average can only make the average worse, the maximum possible value of $\nabla_{K,\omega}$ occurs with $\omega_{21} = \omega_{32} = 0$. Thus, max $\nabla_{K,\omega} = .920$.

To find a lower bound for ∇, we would give the worst component ∇ as large a weight as possible. The worst component ∇ is $\nabla^{(32)} = -.021$. Consider therefore $\omega_{31} = \omega_{32} = 1, \omega_{21} = 0$. Then

$$\nabla_{K,\omega} = \frac{1}{.174 + 0 + .211} [(.174)(.920) + 0 + (.211)(-.021)] = .404$$

Should the remaining component (21) also be given weight in the average? The value of $\nabla^{(21)} = .179$ is less than .404. Therefore, the greater the weight placed on the (21) cells, the lower the overall ∇. Thus, also setting ω_{21} to one, its maximum value allowed by the partial order, we find:

$$\min \nabla_{K,\omega} = \frac{1}{.174 + .034 + .211} [(.174)(.920) + (.034)(.179) + (.211)(-.021)] = .386$$

In summary,

$$.920 \geqslant \nabla_{K,\omega} \geqslant .386$$

for all possible error weights consistent with the partial ordering. Although the two raters are not in perfect agreement, one using the ratings would be glad to find that the two raters have positive success in predicting one another, despite the presence of one negative component ∇. (That this is true for all possible error weights consistent with the ordering does not seem apparent from visual analysis of the table, indicating that even with small tables an important role can be played by statistical prediction analysis.) Nonetheless, the relatively low .386 value of the lower bound might indicate that caution should be exercised when using either rating scale, especially if one thinks that ω_{32} should be relatively large.

Working with kappa has illustrated a general property of ∇. Any ∇ can be expressed as a weighted average of components. This can often be used to advantage when one has ordinal information about the error weights. In addition to the "sensitivity analysis" procedure of establishing bounds on the value of ∇, as in the previous example, one can carry out a more fine-grained analysis by studying how the value of ∇ changes with changes in the numerical values of the error weights. For another illustration analyzing a triangular pattern of error cells with actual survey data, see Hildebrand, Laing, and Rosenthal (1978: section 4.1.2). The general development of ∇ as a weighted average is found in Hildebrand, Laing, and Rosenthal (1977: ch. 3).

In this section, we have developed both the general ∇ measure and the procedure of sensitivity analysis. The methods were applied to the analysis of two conventional measures of association for predictions about single observations. In the remainder of the paper, we extend the application of the methods, first to predictions for pairs of observations, then to joint prediction of quantitative and qualitative variables, and, finally, to multivariate analysis.

3. BIVARIATE PREDICTION FOR PAIRS OF OBSERVATIONS

Computing the Condensed Ordinal Form

To shift from the prediction of single observations to the prediction of pairs, let's return to the bureaucrats. As indicated earlier, any ordinal comparison of two observations on a variable can be condensed into three states: *more, same, less*. The cross-tabulation of the condensed forms of two variables creates 3x3 tables such as Table 3. The first task in the analysis of pair predictions is to compute the entries of Table 3 from the original data, Table 1. Again, we'll treat the party affiliation categories as being ordered along an underlying dimension, perhaps liberalism.

The first step is to compute the row and column totals. Let's start with party affiliation. There are nine *Ind* bureaucrats who are tied on this scale. They can be paired in $9^2 = 81$ different ways. Similarly, there will be 13^2 ties on *Dem* and 9^2 ties on *Rep*. Across all affiliation categories, there are $13^2 + 9^2 + 9^2 = 331$ ties, and these are assigned to the category *same* of the condensed affiliation variable.

The number of ties can be used to compute the number of *more* and *less* pairs. Note that these untied pairs cannot include self-pairs such as (Amy,Amy). Now if Amy has a more liberal party affiliation than Nixman, the pair (Amy,Nixman) will be classified as *more* but the pair (Nixman,Amy) will be classified as *less*. Because of this symmetric counting of pairs, the number of pairs in the *more* category must equal the number assigned to *less*. The total number of pairs is $31^2 = 961$. Since the number of untied pairs is $961 - 331 = 630$, *more* and *less* have the same number of pairs: $630/2 = 315$. This equals the column totals in Table 3.

To get the row (social services) totals, repeat the above procedure. There are $16^2 + 5^2 + 7^2 + 2^2 + 1^2 = 335$ tied pairs. By subtraction, there are $961 - 335 = 626$ untied pairs. By symmetry, there are $626/2 = 313$ pairs in both the *more* and *less* categories.

The center entry in Table 3, corresponding to a tie on both variables, can also be obtained easily. There are 12 bureaucrats that are both *left* and *Dem*. They are tied on both variables. They can be paired in 12^2 ways. There are three *left* and *Ind* bureaucrats for 3^2 pairs. Squaring and summing over all of Table 1 in this manner, compute the total as

$$12^2 + 3^2 + 1^2 + 1^2 + 2^2 + 2^2 + 0^2 + 3^2 + 4^2 +$$

$$0^2 + 1^2 + 1^2 + 0^2 + 0^2 + 1^2 = 191$$

pairs of bureaucrats who are tied on *both* variables, including the 31 self-pairs.

Four more entries in Table 3 can be calculated from symmetry considerations that parallel those invoked for the row and marginal totals. There are 331 tied pairs on affiliation and 191 pairs tied on *both* variables. So, there are 331 – 191 = 140 that are tied on affiliation but not on social services. By symmetry, there are 140/2 = 70 pairs that are *more* on social services but *same* on affiliation and 70 that are *less* on social services but *same* on affiliation. Similarly, 335 – 191 = 144 pairs are tied on social services but untied on affiliation. These split equally, 72 being *more* on affiliation and 72 being *less*.

The only somewhat tricky part in the whole operation involves finding any one of the four corner cells in Table 3. Let's compute the number of *more-more* pairs. The remaining numbers then can be calculated simply.

The 12 *left-Dem* bureaucrats cannot be greater *on both variables* than any of the other bureaucrats in the first (*left*) row or first (*Dem*) column. But they do exhibit the *more-more* relation with all the other bureaucrats in the table. To find these, it is convenient to delete the first row and column, and to add the rest. Schematically, the (1,1) cell contributes

$$\text{12 bureaucrats times the } \textit{sum of} \begin{bmatrix} 2 & 2 \\ 3 & 4 \\ 1 & 1 \\ 0 & 1 \end{bmatrix} = 12 \times 14 = 168 \text{ pairs}$$

There are three *left-Ind* bureaucrats. As was the case for *left-Dem*, the *left-Ind* bureaucrats exhibit the *more-more* relation with all individuals *below and to the right* in the table, contributing

$$\text{3 bureaucrats times the sum of} \begin{bmatrix} 2 \\ 4 \\ 1 \\ 1 \end{bmatrix} = 3 \times 8 = 24 \text{ pairs}$$

The *Rep* column can be ignored since there is no column further to the right. We next turn to the second row. The contributions in the *left-center* row are:

$$1 \textit{ Dem} \text{ times the sum of } \begin{bmatrix} 3 & 4 \\ 1 & 1 \\ 0 & 1 \end{bmatrix} = 1 \times 10 = 10 \text{ pairs}$$

$$2 \textit{ Ind} \text{ times the sum of } \begin{bmatrix} 4 \\ 1 \\ 1 \end{bmatrix} = 2 \times 6 = 12 \text{ pairs}$$

The third row contributions are:

$$0 \textit{ Dem} \text{ times the sum of } \begin{bmatrix} 1 & 1 \\ 0 & 1 \end{bmatrix} = 0 \times 3 = 0 \text{ pairs}$$

$$3 \textit{ Ind} \text{ times the sum of } \begin{bmatrix} 1 \\ 1 \end{bmatrix} = 3 \times 2 = 6 \text{ pairs}$$

The fourth row shows:

$$0 \textit{ Dem} \text{ times the sum of } \begin{bmatrix} 0 & 1 \end{bmatrix} = 0 \text{ pairs}$$

$$1 \textit{ Ind} \text{ times the sum of } \begin{bmatrix} 1 \end{bmatrix} = 1 \text{ pair}$$

The fifth (*right*) row can be ignored since there is no row below it.

In total, there are 168 + 24 + 10 + 12 + 6 + 1 = 221 *more-more* pairs. Now if the pair (Amy,Nixman) is *more-more*, then (Nixman,Amy) must be a *less-less* pair, so there are 221 *less-less* pairs also. Therefore, 313 – 221 – 70 = 22 pairs are *less* on affiliation but *more* on social services and also 22 pairs are *more* on affiliation but *less* on social services. These computations have allowed us to fill all the entries in Table 3.

Prediction in the Condensed Ordinal Form

We are now ready to evaluate some predictions for the condensed form. Six such predictions are shown in Table 12. For all of these predictions, the maximum weight of 1.0 is assigned to occurrences of the "serious" error of observing *less* when *more* is predicted (or vice-versa). Weights less than 1.0 are assigned to less "serious" errors such as observing *same* when *more* is predicted (or vice-versa).

TABLE 12
Four Condensed Form Propositions

Error Table	Proposition	∇ Computation for Data in Table 3

(a-i)

Y^{*2} \ X^{*2}	more	same	less
more			1
same	1/2		1/2
less	1		

$\wp_{d_{yx}}$: more $\rightsquigarrow$ more

same $\rightsquigarrow$ (more, same, or less)

less $\rightsquigarrow$ less

$$\nabla_{d_{yx}} = 1 - \frac{2\left(\frac{22}{961}\right) + 2\left(\frac{1}{2}\right)\left(\frac{72}{961}\right)}{2\left(\frac{313}{961}\right)\left(\frac{315}{961}\right) + 2\left(\frac{1}{2}\right)\left(\frac{335}{961}\right)\left(\frac{315}{961}\right)}$$

$$= 1 - \frac{.121}{.328} = .632$$

(a-ii)

Y^{*2} \ X^{*2}	more	same	less
more	1		
same	1/2		1/2
less			1

$\wp_{-d_{yx}}$: more $\rightsquigarrow$ less

same $\rightsquigarrow$ (more, same, or less)

less $\rightsquigarrow$ more

$$\nabla_{-d_{yx}} = 1 - \frac{2\left(\frac{221}{961}\right) + 2\left(\frac{1}{2}\right)\left(\frac{72}{961}\right)}{2\left(\frac{313}{961}\right)\left(\frac{315}{961}\right) + 2\left(\frac{1}{2}\right)\left(\frac{335}{961}\right)\left(\frac{315}{961}\right)}$$

$$= 1 - \frac{.535}{.328} = -.632$$

TABLE 12 (Continued)

Error Table	Proposition	∇ Computation for Data in Table 3

(b-i)

Error Table (X^{*2} across, Y^{*2} down):

Y^{*2} \ X^{*2}	more	same	less
more		1/2	1
same			
less	1	1/2	

Proposition: $\wp_{d_{y.x}}$: more $\leadsto$ more or same; same $\leadsto$ same; less $\leadsto$ same or less

$$\nabla_{d_{y.x}} = 1 - \frac{2\left(\frac{1}{2}\right)\left(\frac{70}{961}\right) + 2\left(\frac{22}{961}\right)}{2\left(\frac{1}{2}\right)\left(\frac{313}{961}\right)\left(\frac{331}{961}\right) + 2\left(\frac{313}{961}\right)\left(\frac{315}{961}\right)}$$

$$= 1 - \frac{.119}{.326} = .636$$

(c-i)

Error Table (X^{*2} across, Y^{*2} down):

Y^{*2} \ X^{*2}	more	same	less
more		1/4	1
same	1/4		1/4
less	1	1/4	

Proposition: $\wp_d$: more $\leadsto$ more; same $\leadsto$ same; less $\leadsto$ less

$$\nabla_d = 1 - \frac{2\left(\frac{1}{4}\right)\left(\frac{70}{961}\right) + 2\left(\frac{22}{961}\right) + 2\left(\frac{1}{4}\right)\left(\frac{72}{961}\right)}{2\left(\frac{1}{4}\right)\left(\frac{313}{961}\right)\left(\frac{331}{961}\right) + 2\left(\frac{313}{961}\right)\left(\frac{315}{961}\right) + 2\left(\frac{1}{4}\right)\left(\frac{335}{961}\right)\left(\frac{315}{961}\right)}$$

$$= 1 - \frac{.120}{.327} = .634$$

Note: Tables contain weights for error cells. Success cells ($\omega_{ij} = 0$) are blank.

Table 12 also shows the calculation of ∇ for the data in Table 3. Recall that

$$\nabla_{\mathcal{P}} = 1 - (\text{Observed Errors}/\text{Expected Errors})$$

Applying the error weights of Table 12(a-i) to the data in Table 3, we find that the (weighted) observed errors, as proportions, are

$$\left(\frac{22}{961}\right) + \left(\frac{22}{961}\right) + \left(\frac{1}{2}\right)\left(\frac{72}{961}\right) + \left(\frac{1}{2}\right)\left(\frac{72}{961}\right)$$

This term equals the numerator of the first right hand term in the $\nabla_{d_{yx}}$ calculation in (a-i).

Similarly, we calculate the expected error proportion for each error cell by multiplying the corresponding marginal proportions. We then multiply these proportions by the appropriate error weights and sum, to obtain

$$\left(\frac{313}{961}\right)\left(\frac{315}{961}\right) + \left(\frac{313}{961}\right)\left(\frac{315}{961}\right) + \left(\frac{1}{2}\right)\left(\frac{335}{961}\right)\left(\frac{315}{961}\right) + \left(\frac{1}{2}\right)\left(\frac{335}{961}\right)\left(\frac{315}{961}\right)$$

This term equals the denominator of the first right hand term in the $\nabla_{d_{yx}}$ calculation in the table.

Note that if one cell is an error cell, its opposite cell in the table is also an error cell and has the same weight. Examples include: In Table 12(a-i), the *less-more* cell has a weight of 1.0, matching the *more-less* cell; in Table 12 (b-i) the cells *more-same* and *less-same* are both error cells with weights of 1/2; in Table 12(c-i), the *same-more* and *same-less* cells are both weighted 1/4. This parallels our finding above that these cells, because of symmetry, must have an equal number of pairs. In general, condensed forms of any table always exhibit this *radial symmetry* about the center cell. Because of this symmetry, any two symmetric cells must either both be successes or both be errors. If they are errors, the error weights must be identical.

Pairs in the *more-more* and *less-less* cells are termed *concordant* since the observation pairs are ordered identically on both Y and X. Similarly, the *more-less* and *less-more* pairs are termed *discordant*. Note that the ∇ values displayed in Tables 12(a-i, a-ii) are equal in magnitude but opposite in sign. The predictions in each pair (a-i, a-ii) differ only by flipping the roles of the concordant and discordant pairs. Flipping the roles of concordant and discordant, we could also develop tables b-ii and c-ii as comparisons to b-i and c-i in Table 12. The (i) predictions are representations of "the more X, the more Y"; the (ii) predictions are representations of "the more X, the less Y." Since the magnitudes of both members of the (i-ii) pairs must be equal and since ∇ has a maximum value of 1.0, these special predictions must all have a minimum value of –1.0. The ∇ for the (i) predictions equals

(a) Somers' (1962) d_{yx},
(b) Kim's (1971) $d_{y.x}$, and
(c) Kim's (1971) symmetric d.

(In the next section, we develop these measures in greater detail.) All the measures shown in Table 12 were developed with X as the independent variable. For the first two "asymmetric" measures, Somers and Kim have proposed corresponding measures when X is the dependent variable, indicated by reversing the position of the subscripts. It can readily be shown that $d_{xy} = d_{y.x}$ and $d_{x.y} = d_{yx}$.

One way to use these measures is to compute them using prediction (i). Then, if the value is negative, ex post one can change the sign of the measure and adopt prediction (ii) as an interpretation of the data. One can also use the measure in an a priori sense, reporting a negative value as a strong indication of prediction failure.

In the case of Table 12, the magnitudes of the three measures show little variation. Results like these occur rather often, but wider variation can readily occur. In order to give some simplified computing formulas for these established measures, we first develop the general probability notation for the condensed form.

General Development of the Condensed Form

The entries for the condensed form are shown symbolically in Table 13. The symbol $P(\underset{\sim}{C})$ refers to the probability of concordance, $P(\underset{\sim}{D})$ to discordance, $P(\underset{\sim}{T}_X)$ to a tie on X, $P(\underset{\sim}{T}_{\bar{Y}X})$ to a tie on X but not on Y, $P(\bar{\underset{\sim}{T}}_X)$ to the probability of not being tied on X, etc. The entries in Table 13 can be calculated from the entries in an RxC table of population probabilities as:

$$P(\underset{\sim}{T}_Y) = \sum_{i=1}^{R} P_{i.}^2, \qquad P(\bar{\underset{\sim}{T}}_Y) = 1 - P(\underset{\sim}{T}_Y)$$

$$P(\underset{\sim}{T}_X) = \sum_{j=1}^{C} P_{.j}^2, \qquad P(\bar{\underset{\sim}{T}}_X) = 1 - P(\underset{\sim}{T}_X)$$

$$P(\underset{\sim}{T}_{YX}) = \sum_{i=1}^{R}\sum_{j=1}^{C} P_{ij}^2$$

$$P(\underset{\sim}{T}_{Y\bar{X}}) = P(\underset{\sim}{T}_Y) - P(\underset{\sim}{T}_{YX})$$

$$P(\underset{\sim}{T}_{\bar{Y}X}) = P(\underset{\sim}{T}_X) - P(\underset{\sim}{T}_{YX})$$

TABLE 13
The General Condensed Ordinal Form

		X^{*2} more	X^{*2} same	X^{*2} less	
Y^{*2}	more	$\frac{1}{2}P(\underset{\sim}{C})$	$\frac{1}{2}P(\underset{\sim}{T}_{\bar{Y}X})$	$\frac{1}{2}P(\underset{\sim}{D})$	$\frac{1}{2}P(\underset{\sim}{\bar{T}}_{Y})$
	same	$\frac{1}{2}P(\underset{\sim}{T}_{Y\bar{X}})$	$P(\underset{\sim}{T}_{YX})$	$\frac{1}{2}P(\underset{\sim}{T}_{Y\bar{X}})$	$P(\underset{\sim}{T}_{Y})$
	less	$\frac{1}{2}P(\underset{\sim}{D})$	$\frac{1}{2}P(\underset{\sim}{T}_{\bar{Y}X})$	$\frac{1}{2}P(\underset{\sim}{C})$	$\frac{1}{2}P(\underset{\sim}{\bar{T}}_{Y})$
		$\frac{1}{2}P(\underset{\sim}{\bar{T}}_{X})$	$P(\underset{\sim}{T}_{X})$	$\frac{1}{2}P(\underset{\sim}{\bar{T}}_{X})$	1.0

$$P(\underset{\sim}{C}) = 2\sum_{i=1}^{R-1}\sum_{j=1}^{C-1}\sum_{g=i+1}^{R}\sum_{h=j+1}^{C} P_{ij}P_{gh}$$

$$P(\underset{\sim}{D}) = 1 - P(\underset{\sim}{C}) - P(\underset{\sim}{T}_{Y\bar{X}}) - P(\underset{\sim}{T}_{\bar{Y}X}) - P(\underset{\sim}{T}_{YX})$$

Note that g is just an alternate index for the rows, h for the columns.[2] As an exercise, convert Table 1 to probabilities and use the above formula to compute the condensed ordinal form. As a check, convert Table 3 to probabilities.

Using the above general expressions for the condensed form, the d type measures may be expressed as:

$$d_{yx} = d_{x.y} = \frac{P(\underset{\sim}{C}) - P(\underset{\sim}{D})}{P(\underset{\sim}{\bar{T}}_{X})} = \frac{P(\underset{\sim}{C}) - P(\underset{\sim}{D})}{P(\underset{\sim}{C}) + P(\underset{\sim}{D}) + P(\underset{\sim}{T}_{Y\bar{X}})}$$

$$d_{xy} = d_{y.x} = \frac{P(\underset{\sim}{C}) - P(\underset{\sim}{D})}{P(\underset{\sim}{\bar{T}}_{Y})} = \frac{P(\underset{\sim}{C}) - P(\underset{\sim}{D})}{P(\underset{\sim}{C}) + P(\underset{\sim}{D}) + P(\underset{\sim}{T}_{\bar{Y}X})}$$

$$d = \frac{P(\underset{\sim}{C}) - P(\underset{\sim}{D})}{\frac{1}{2}[P(\underset{\sim}{\bar{T}}_{X}) + P(\underset{\sim}{\bar{T}}_{Y})]} = \frac{P(\underset{\sim}{C}) - P(\underset{\sim}{D})}{\frac{1}{2}[2P(\underset{\sim}{C}) + 2P(\underset{\sim}{D}) + P(\underset{\sim}{T}_{Y\bar{X}}) + P(\underset{\sim}{T}_{\bar{Y}X})]}$$

From Table 3, for example,

$$d_{yx} = \frac{2(221/961 - 22/961)}{2(315/961)} = .632$$

as before.

Expressed in this form, the d measures differ only in the denominators. In effect they are identical except for how they handle ties. In the asymmetric measures (d_{yx} and $d_{y.x}$) Somers adjusts the difference between concordance and discordance probabilities on the basis of independent variable ties while Kim adjusts using the dependent variable. Kim's symmetric measure (d) simply averages the two adjusting factors; hence, as illustrated in Table 12, the value of d must lie half-way between the two asymmetric measures.

Once one has the condensed form, these measures are easy to compute. That appears to be their primary advantage over other ∇ measures for the condensed form. One ought to be willing, however, to sacrifice computational facility if alternative error weights are more attuned to research purposes.

Sensitivity Analysis of the Condensed Ordinal Form

When one's research hypothesis is simply "The more X, the more Y," there is in fact no compelling reason to choose one of the three d measures. It is clear that concordant pairs and pairs simultaneously tied on both variables do not represent errors for this prediction. In contrast, discordant pairs are the most serious form of error and ought to receive the maximum error weight, $\omega_{\underset{\sim}{D}} = 1$. Pairs tied on only one variable are less serious errors. The two weights $\omega_{\underset{\sim}{T}Y\bar{X}}$ and $\omega_{\underset{\sim}{T}\bar{Y}X}$ ought not to exceed $\omega_{\underset{\sim}{D}}$, but their relative weights are not indicated by the hypothesis. Which numerical values will be given to $\omega_{\underset{\sim}{T}Y\bar{X}}$ and $\omega_{\underset{\sim}{T}\bar{Y}X}$ are left to the investigator's judgment.

In summary, for evaluating "The more X, the more Y" in the full condensed form, the partial order of error weights is identical to that found for the analysis of kappa in 3x3 tables of single observations, as illustrated in Figure 2.

Performing the sensitivity analysis for the data in Table 3, first compute the ∇ and U statistics for the component predictions:

$$\nabla_{\underset{\sim}{D}} = .786 \qquad U_{\underset{\sim}{D}} = .214$$

$$\nabla_{\underset{\sim}{T}Y\bar{X}} = .344 \qquad U_{\underset{\sim}{T}Y\bar{X}} = .229$$

$$\nabla_{\underset{\sim}{T}\bar{Y}X} = .351 \qquad U_{\underset{\sim}{T}\bar{Y}X} = .224$$

To find the maximum possible value of ∇ consistent with the partial order of weights, note that $\nabla_{\underset{\sim}{D}}$, which must have the highest error weight, is the largest of the three ∇'s. Therefore, max $\nabla = .786$. In this case, as in the earlier

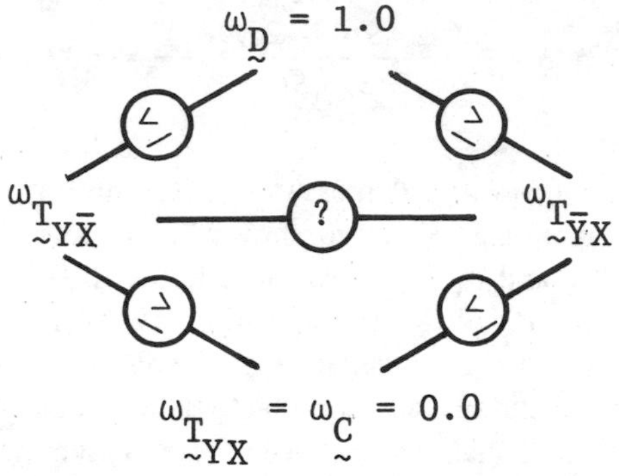

Figure 2: Partial Order of Error Weights for Condensed Ordinal Form

case concerning kappa, both of the other components must receive an error weight of 1.0 in computing

$$\min \nabla = \frac{1}{.214 + .229 + .224} \times [(.214)(.786) + (.229)(.344) + (.224)(.351)] = .488$$

Therefore

$$.786 \geqslant \nabla \geqslant .488$$

for all sets of error weights consistent with the research hypothesis. Reporting a range of values like the above appears to be preferable to any arbitrary selection of a single measure.

Restricting the Domain of the Prediction by Excluding All Ties

The Somers and Kim measures presented above recognize the typical prevalence of ties in ordinal data and allow for their occurrence within the prediction domain. Goodman and Kruskal (1954) adopt the extreme solution to the problem of ties: they exclude all tied pairs from the prediction domain. To discard all ties, simply form a new condensed form table with the middle (*same*) row and column deleted. The probability of not having a tie is $P(\underset{\sim}{\bar{T}}) = P(\underset{\sim}{C}) + P(\underset{\sim}{D})$. If the probabilities in the new domain are to sum to 1.0, all the relevant old probabilities have to be divided by $P(\underset{\sim}{\bar{T}})$. The result is shown in Table 14. The 50-50 marginals are another consequence of radial symmetry. Consider the prediction $\mathcal{Y}$: *more* $\leftrightsquigarrow$ *more*. Again, the radial symmetry im-

TABLE 14
The Condensed Form When the Domain Excludes Ties

		X^{*2}		
		more	less	
Y^{*2}	more	$\frac{P(\underset{\sim}{C})}{2P(\underset{\sim}{\bar{T}})}$	$\frac{P(\underset{\sim}{D})}{2P(\underset{\sim}{\bar{T}})}$	.5
	less	$\frac{P(\underset{\sim}{D})}{2P(\underset{\sim}{\bar{T}})}$	$\frac{P(\underset{\sim}{C})}{2P(\underset{\sim}{\bar{T}})}$	.5
		.5	.5	1.0

$$P(\underset{\sim}{\bar{T}}) = P(\underset{\sim}{C}) + P(\underset{\sim}{D})$$

Note: Shaded cells indicate errors for prediction underlying gamma, excluding all ties: more $\leftrightsquigarrow$ more.

plies that equal weights should be given to the errors (*more-less* and *less-more*). Applying the $\nabla_{\wp}$ model for this prediction,

$$\nabla_{\mathscr{G}} = 1 - \frac{\frac{1}{2}P(\underset{\sim}{D})/P(\underset{\sim}{\bar{T}}) + \frac{1}{2}P(\underset{\sim}{D})/P(\underset{\sim}{\bar{T}})}{(1/2)(1/2) + (1/2)(1/2)}$$

$$= \frac{P(\underset{\sim}{C}) - P(\underset{\sim}{D})}{P(\underset{\sim}{\bar{T}})} = \frac{P(\underset{\sim}{C}) - P(\underset{\sim}{D})}{P(\underset{\sim}{C}) + P(\underset{\sim}{D})} = \text{gamma}$$

where gamma is a well-known measure of ordinal association developed by Goodman and Kruskal (1954). Thus gamma is a ∇ measure for the *more* $\leftrightsquigarrow$ *more* prediction after all tied pairs have been discarded. The $\nabla_{\wp}$ measure for the opposite prediction for this domain, *more* $\leftrightsquigarrow$ *less,* equals the negative of gamma. Recognizing the symmetry in the 2x2 cross classification of Table 14, these are the only two predictions of interest for this narrowly restricted domain. Moreover, the symmetry also implies that all error events should have the same weight in this case, so there is no need for sensitivity analysis.

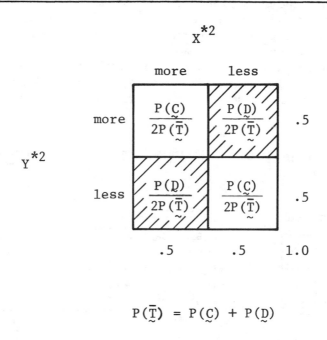

For the data of Table 3, gamma = .819. This is one instance of a universally true fact that can be proved simply by comparing the expressions for gamma and the d measures: gamma must always have a larger numerical value than any of the d measures. By treating much of the data (ties) as irrelevant, gamma achieves large and perhaps misleading measures of error reduction. For this reason, even though it appeared earlier in the literature and, as a consequence, has been used more widely than any of the d measures, gamma seems inadequate for evaluating "The more X, the more Y." A particularly striking example is the following simple 2x2 table and its condensed ordinal forms with and without ties:

2 x 2 Table

		X	
		x	$\bar{x}$
Y	y	.1	.0
	$\bar{y}$	.8	.1

Condensed Form With Ties

		X^{*2}		
		more	same	less
Y^{*2}	more	.01	.08	.00
	same	.08	.66	.08
	less	.00	.08	.01

Condensed Form Without Ties

		X^{*2}	
		more	less
Y^{*2}	more	.5	0
	less	0	.5

Clearly Y does not really increase strongly with X. When x occurs, 8/9 of the observations are still $\bar{y}$. Yet, for this table, gamma = 1.0. In contrast, all three d measures equal .111. For a 2x2 table, perhaps the most natural way to test "The more X, the more Y" and similar statements is to use the prediction $x \leftrightsquigarrow y$ for single observations with equally weighted errors. Then

$$\nabla_{x \leftrightsquigarrow y} = 1 - \frac{.8 + .0}{(.9)(.9) + (.1)(.1)} = .024$$

This value contrasts sharply with the "strong" positive association gamma "captures" after it excludes fully 98% of the observation pairs.

Restricting the Domain by Eliminating Ties on One Variable

We have criticized gamma for evaluating a prediction that is too imprecise because it applies only to a possibly small subset of the data for the entire condensed form. We can substantiate this criticism further by comparing gamma and the asymmetric d measures in a common domain. Both gamma and the asymmetric measures can also be developed as ∇ measures when the domain excludes ties on only one variable. That is, once we specify the appropriate error weights for this domain, then the corresponding ∇ measure is equivalent mathematically to the ordinal measure. Our discussion covers only exclusion of ties on the independent variable although the parallel treatment of the dependent variable is shown in Table 15.

When independent variable (X) ties are excluded, as shown in Table 15, concordant pairs are again successes for "The more X, the more Y" and discordant pairs errors with weight 1.0. We can regard ties on the dependent variable as less severe errors, so that

$$1 = \omega_{\underset{\sim}{D}} \geqslant \omega_{\underset{\sim}{T}_{Y\bar{X}}} \geqslant \omega_{\underset{\sim}{C}} = 0$$

Let us first examine the component $\nabla_{\underset{\sim}{T}_{Y\bar{X}}}$ for the prediction *more* ⇝ (*more* or *less*) & *less* ⇝ (*more* or *less*). Since, in the restricted domain excluding all X-ties, this component's error cells fill an entire row, it is a totally *undifferentiated* prediction which cannot possibly take advantage of information on the independent variable state. The usual computation of ∇ in fact shows that $\nabla_{\underset{\sim}{T}_{Y\bar{X}}}$ always equals zero if it is defined.

As to the second component identifying only discordant pairs as errors,

$$\nabla_{\underset{\sim}{D}} = 1 - \frac{P(\underset{\sim}{D})/P(\bar{\underset{\sim}{T}}_X)}{\frac{1}{2}\,[P(\underset{\sim}{C}) + P(\underset{\sim}{D})]\,/P(\bar{\underset{\sim}{T}}_X)} = \frac{P(\underset{\sim}{C}) - P(\underset{\sim}{D})}{P(\underset{\sim}{C}) + P(\underset{\sim}{D})} = \text{gamma}$$

If the ties component is assigned an error weight of 1/2 and the components combined, given $\omega_{\underset{\sim}{T}_{Y\bar{X}}} = 1/2$ and $\omega_{\underset{\sim}{D}} = 1$, then

$$\nabla = \frac{1}{\omega_{\underset{\sim}{D}} U_{\underset{\sim}{D}} + \omega_{\underset{\sim}{T}_{Y\bar{X}}} U_{\underset{\sim}{T}_{Y\bar{X}}}} [\omega_{\underset{\sim}{D}} U_{\underset{\sim}{D}} \nabla_{\underset{\sim}{D}} + \omega_{\underset{\sim}{T}_{Y\bar{X}}} U_{\underset{\sim}{T}_{Y\bar{X}}} \nabla_{\underset{\sim}{T}_{Y\bar{X}}}]$$

$$= \frac{1}{\dfrac{\frac{1}{2}\,[P(\underset{\sim}{C}) + P(\underset{\sim}{D})] + \frac{1}{2}\,P(\underset{\sim}{T}_{Y\bar{X}})}{P(\bar{\underset{\sim}{T}}_X)}} \left[\left[\frac{\frac{1}{2}\,[P(\underset{\sim}{C}) + P(\underset{\sim}{D})]}{P(\bar{\underset{\sim}{T}}_X)}\right]\left[\frac{P(\underset{\sim}{C}) - P(\underset{\sim}{D})}{P(\underset{\sim}{C}) + P(\underset{\sim}{D})}\right] + 0\right]$$

$$= \frac{P(\underset{\sim}{C}) - P(\underset{\sim}{D})}{P(\underset{\sim}{C}) + P(\underset{\sim}{D}) + P(\underset{\sim}{T}_{Y\bar{X}})} = \frac{P(\underset{\sim}{C}) - P(\underset{\sim}{D})}{P(\bar{\underset{\sim}{T}}_X)} = d_{yx}$$

Our development of d_{yx} in the above expression shows that the ties which gamma ignores do not affect the *sign* of overall ∇. The sign depends on $P(\underset{\sim}{C})$ –

TABLE 15
Prediction Analysis When the Domain Excludes Ties on Only One Variable

Ties excluded on:

X^{*2}

Condensed Form of X^{*2}

Probabilities:

Y^{*2}	more	less	
more	$\frac{P(\underset{\sim}{C})}{2P(\underset{\sim}{\bar{T}}_X)}$	$\frac{P(\underset{\sim}{D})}{2P(\underset{\sim}{\bar{T}}_X)}$	$\frac{P(\underset{\sim}{\bar{T}})}{2P(\underset{\sim}{\bar{T}}_X)}$
same	$\frac{P(T_{\underset{\sim}{Y}\bar{X}})}{2P(\underset{\sim}{\bar{T}}_X)}$	$\frac{P(T_{\underset{\sim}{Y}\bar{X}})}{2P(\underset{\sim}{\bar{T}}_X)}$	$\frac{P(T_{\underset{\sim}{Y}\bar{X}})}{P(\underset{\sim}{\bar{T}}_X)}$
less	$\frac{P(\underset{\sim}{D})}{2P(\underset{\sim}{\bar{T}}_X)}$	$\frac{P(\underset{\sim}{C})}{2P(\underset{\sim}{\bar{T}}_X)}$	$\frac{P(\underset{\sim}{\bar{T}})}{2P(\underset{\sim}{\bar{T}}_X)}$
	.5	.5	

Error Weights:

Y^{*2}	more	less
more	$\omega_{\underset{\sim}{C}}$	$\omega_{\underset{\sim}{D}}$
same	$\omega_{T_{\underset{\sim}{Y}\bar{X}}}$	$\omega_{T_{\underset{\sim}{Y}\bar{X}}}$
less	$\omega_{\underset{\sim}{D}}$	$\omega_{\underset{\sim}{C}}$

Error Weights	Measure
$\omega_{\underset{\sim}{D}} = 1.0,\ \omega_{\underset{\sim}{C}} = \omega_{T_{\underset{\sim}{\bar{Y}}X}} = 0.0$	Gamma
$\omega_{\underset{\sim}{D}} = 1.0,\ \omega_{T_{\underset{\sim}{Y}\bar{X}}} = 0.5,\ \omega_{\underset{\sim}{C}} = 0.0$	Somers' d_{yx} (= Kim's $d_{x.y}$ if Y^{*2} independent variable).

Y^{*2}

Condensed Form of X^{*2}

Probabilities:

Y^{*2}	more	same	less	
more	$\frac{P(\underset{\sim}{C})}{2P(\underset{\sim}{\bar{T}}_Y)}$	$\frac{P(T_{\bar{Y}X})}{2P(\underset{\sim}{\bar{T}}_Y)}$	$\frac{P(\underset{\sim}{D})P}{2P(\underset{\sim}{\bar{T}}_Y)}$	.5
less	$\frac{P(\underset{\sim}{D})}{2P(\underset{\sim}{\bar{T}}_Y)}$	$\frac{P(T_{\underset{\sim}{\bar{Y}}X})}{2P(\underset{\sim}{\bar{T}}_Y)}$	$\frac{P(\underset{\sim}{C})}{2P(\underset{\sim}{\bar{T}}_Y)}$	.5
	$\frac{P(\underset{\sim}{\bar{T}})}{2P(\underset{\sim}{\bar{T}}_Y)}$	$\frac{P(T_{\underset{\sim}{\bar{Y}}X})}{P(\underset{\sim}{\bar{T}}_Y)}$	$\frac{P(\underset{\sim}{\bar{T}})}{2P(\underset{\sim}{\bar{T}}_Y)}$	

Error Weights:

Y^{*2}	more	same	less
more	$\omega_{\underset{\sim}{C}}$	$\omega_{T_{\underset{\sim}{\bar{Y}}X}}$	$\omega_{\underset{\sim}{D}}$
less	$\omega_{\underset{\sim}{D}}$	$\omega_{T_{\underset{\sim}{\bar{Y}}X}}$	$\omega_{\underset{\sim}{C}}$

Error Weights	Measure
$\omega_{\underset{\sim}{D}} = 1.0,\ \omega_{\underset{\sim}{C}} = \omega_{T_{\underset{\sim}{\bar{Y}}X}} = 0.0$	Gamma
$\omega_{\underset{\sim}{D}} = 1.0,\ \omega_{T_{\underset{\sim}{\bar{Y}}X}} = 0.5,\ \omega_{\underset{\sim}{C}} = 0.0$	Somers' d_{xy} (= Kim's $d_{y.x}$ if X^{*2} independent variable).

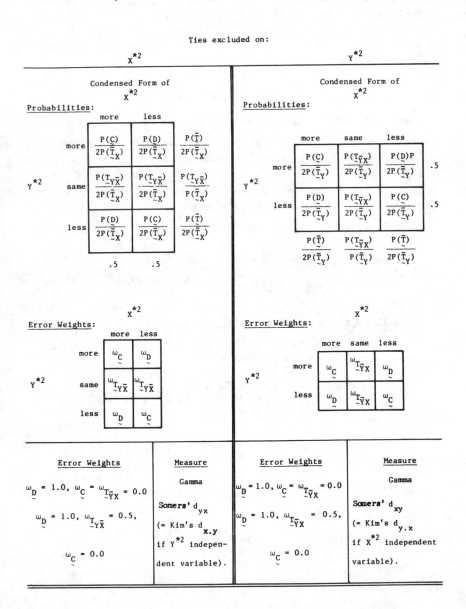

$P(\underset{\sim}{D})$. Despite the fact that the ties component can never be successful, it does serve as an appropriate way of dampening the magnitude of gamma ($\nabla_{\underset{\sim}{D}}$). For example, consider the following two tables for the restricted condensed form:

.5	.0
.0	.0
.0	.5

.2	.0
.3	.3
.0	.2

Clearly the left-hand table permits stronger prediction of relative order. Gamma, nonetheless, is 1.0 for both tables. Since there are no ties, d_{yx} also equals 1.0 in the first table. In contrast, discounting for the ties in the second table, we have $d_{yx} = 0.4$ there.

Again, if only ordinal specifications of the error weights can be justified, then we advocate sensitivity analysis rather than relying solely on either d_{yx} or gamma. Consider a sensitivity analysis of the condensed ordinal form omitting ties on the independent variable. The value of ∇ for "The *more* X, the *more* Y" in this domain is a weighted average of gamma ($\nabla_{\underset{\sim}{D}}$) and $\nabla_{\underset{\sim}{T}X\bar{Y}}$, and we have shown that the latter must be zero. Therefore, if gamma is positive, then it is the maximum possible value of ∇ for this proposition. Omitting ties on X from the data of Table 3, we have $\nabla_{\underset{\sim}{D}} = .819$. Also, given $\nabla_{\underset{\sim}{D}} > 0$, the minimum value of ∇ for the proposition occurs when $\omega_{\tilde{T}Y\bar{X}} = 1$. Thus, omitting ties on X from the data of Table 3 yields $.434 \leqslant \nabla \leqslant .819$. If, instead, ties on the dependent variable are eliminated, then the corresponding bounds are $.520 \leqslant \nabla \leqslant .819$.

Eliminating a Cell Rather than a Row or Column from the Domain

Another approach to ties has been followed by Wilson (1974), who excludes pairs tied on *both* variables as irrelevant. Otherwise, as shown in Table 16, his prediction is the same as that for Kim's symmetric d, except the error weights for cells involving ties are 1/2 rather than 1/4. If we eliminate the center cell and renormalize the probabilities, we have the structure shown in Table 16.

Wilson's approach, as seen in the table, regards a single cell as irrelevant, rather than an entire row or column, as with gamma. Analyzing this type of prediction presents important conceptual and technical difficulties. We will skip these issues here, referring the reader to Hildebrand, Laing, and Rosenthal (1977, ch. 4). By applying the set-by-set procedure discussed there to Wilson's prediction for the error weights shown in Table 16, it can be shown that the resulting ∇ measure equals the measure proposed by Wilson and also by Deuchler (1914):

TABLE 16
Prediction With a Hole

Condensed Form With (same,same) Excluded from the Domain

		X^{*2}			
		more	same	less	
Y^{*2}	more	$\frac{P(\underset{\sim}{C})}{2A}$	$\frac{P(\underset{\sim}{T}_{\bar{Y}X})}{2A}$	$\frac{P(\underset{\sim}{D})}{2A}$	$\frac{P(\bar{\underset{\sim}{T}}_Y)}{2A}$
	same	$\frac{P(\underset{\sim}{T}_{Y\bar{X}})}{2A}$	irrelevant cell	$\frac{P(\underset{\sim}{T}_{Y\bar{X}})}{2A}$	$\frac{P(\underset{\sim}{T}_{Y\bar{X}})}{A}$
	less	$\frac{P(\underset{\sim}{D})}{2A}$	$\frac{P(\underset{\sim}{T}_{\bar{Y}X})}{2A}$	$\frac{P(\underset{\sim}{C})}{2A}$	$\frac{P(\bar{\underset{\sim}{T}}_Y)}{2A}$
		$\frac{P(\bar{\underset{\sim}{T}}_X)}{2A}$	$\frac{P(\underset{\sim}{T}_{\bar{Y}X})}{A}$	$\frac{P(\bar{\underset{\sim}{T}}_X)}{2A}$	1.0

Error Matrix for Wilson's e

		X^{*2}		
		more	same	less
Y^{*2}	more	0	1/2	1
	same	1/2	irrelevant cell	1/2
	less	1	1/2	0

Note: $A = 1 - P(\underset{\sim}{T}_{YX})$.

$$e = 1 - \frac{[P(\underset{\sim}{D}) + (1/2)P(\underset{\sim}{T}_{Y\bar{X}}) + (1/2)P(\underset{\sim}{T}_{\bar{Y}X})] / [1 - P(\underset{\sim}{T}_{YX})]}{1/2}$$

$$= \frac{P(\underset{\sim}{C}) - P(\underset{\sim}{D})}{1 - P(\underset{\sim}{T}_{YX})}$$

By looking at the denominator of the last expression for e, it can be seen that e is more conservative than either the d measure or, of course, gamma. For the data of Table 3, e = .517. The conservative behavior of e reflects the high error weight placed on pairs tied on one variable. The asymmetric d measures include only two of these cells as errors while Kim's symmetric measure weights the four such cells 1/4 rather than 1/2.

Comparing Predictions Across Domains

Within a given domain, we can evaluate predictions in terms of prediction success (∇) and precision (U). Recall that U simply equals the "expected" error rate, that is, the denominator of the ratio in the expression for ∇. If one prediction has higher values than another on both of these dimensions, then the first prediction is said to dominate the second. Very frequently, however, there is a trade-off between prediction success and precision. One may have to sacrifice precision to get a high ∇ value. The same remark can be applied to a given population even when predictions apply to different domains within that population. The only change is that we have to correct the precision measure to reflect the different population proportions included within the domain:

$$U^c = U \times \text{proportion of population in domain}$$

For example, when gamma is developed for the domain that excludes all ties, we found earlier that $U_{gamma} = (.5 \times .5) + (.5 \times .5) = .5$. Therefore $U^c_{gamma} = .5P(\bar{\underset{\sim}{T}})$.

We can apply U^c to compare some conventional measures of ordinal association. We have already seen that gamma is always greater than or equal to d_{yx} which in turn is always greater than or equal to e. There is a direct trade-off, however, in terms of precision since

$$U^c_{gamma} = .5P(\bar{\underset{\sim}{T}}) \leqslant U^c_{d_{yx}} = .5P(\bar{\underset{\sim}{T}}_X) \leqslant U^c_e = .5[1 - P(\underset{\sim}{T}_{YX})]$$

One can therefore either pick a measure for a relatively successful but imprecise prediction or vice versa. Since reporting prediction precision is almost always omitted, unfortunately, from the presentation of research results, researchers have had an incentive to use gamma.

Concordance and Discordance: Looking Backwards

As mentioned previously, the conventional condensed form measures can all be viewed as attempts to adjust the difference between the probability of concordant pairs and the probability of discordant pairs, $P(\underset{\sim}{C}) - P(\underset{\sim}{D})$. This quantity, Kruskal (1958) indicates, first began to appear in statistics around the turn of the century. It is commonly known as Kendall's (1962) tau. (Not to be confused with Kendall's τ_b, which we discuss in a later section.) The measure was originally thought of as being applied to populations without ties, excluding self-pairs from the prediction's domain. For the case of ties, Kruskal views gamma as the generalization of tau. Rather than changing the domain as for gamma, another approach is to maintain the full domain of the condensed form and seek a prediction whose ∇-value is $P(\underset{\sim}{C}) - P(\underset{\sim}{D})$. When $\omega_{\underset{\sim}{D}} = 1.0$, $\omega_{\underset{\sim}{T}\bar{Y}X} = \omega_{\underset{\sim}{T}Y\bar{X}} = \omega_{\underset{\sim}{T}YX} = 1/2$, $\omega_{\underset{\sim}{C}} = 0$, we find that

$$\nabla = tau = P(\underset{\sim}{C}) - P(\underset{\sim}{D}),\ U_{tau} = .5$$

The underlying prediction does not seem appropriate to evaluate "The *more* X, the *more* Y" since it regards simultaneous ties as errors. In other contexts, it seems appropriate. For example, suppose, as in various questions asked by the Survey Research Center of the University of Michigan, two voters are asked to assign each of a dozen or so candidates to one of the 101 positions on a 0 to 100 "thermometer" scale as an indication of how "warm" they feel towards each candidate. If the a priori prediction were both (a) that neither voter assigns two or more candidates to the same scale position, and (b) that both voters rank the candidates identically (although perhaps using different scores), then tau is a reasonable measure. In any event, tau will always be the least "successful" but most precise of the $P(\underset{\sim}{C}) - P(\underset{\sim}{D})$ family. For the data in Table 3, tau = 2[(221/961) – (22/961)] = .414.

One More Normalization: Kendall's τ_c

Another method of normalizing the basic term $P(\underset{\sim}{C}) - P(\underset{\sim}{D})$ is to multiply by the fraction M/M–1, where M is the minimum of R and C. This gives

$$\tau_c = \frac{M}{M-1}\,[P(\underset{\sim}{C}) - P(\underset{\sim}{D})]$$

The motivation for this correction is that M–1/M is the maximum possible value (Kendall, 1962) for $P(\underset{\sim}{C}) - P(\underset{\sim}{D})$ in an RxC table. This normalization is a convenient way of bounding a "tau" statistic between –1 and +1, but the procedure appears ad hoc from the viewpoint of prediction analysis. We have not been able to interpret τ_c within the "del" framework applied to all the other measures considered in this paper.

Kendall's τ_b^2: Mixed Strategy Prediction for the Condensed Form and Analogies to Prediction for Quantitative Variables

Kendall's (1962) τ_b^2 is a measure intimately related to the $P(\underset{\sim}{C}) - P(\underset{\sim}{D})$ family, as is evident in the expression

$$\tau_b^2 = d_{yx}d_{xy} = \frac{[P(\underset{\sim}{C}) - P(\underset{\sim}{D})]^2}{P(\underset{\sim}{\overline{T}}_Y)P(\underset{\sim}{\overline{T}}_X)}$$

The Linear Model Analogy: The Somers-Hawkes (Somers, 1968, 1974; Hawkes, 1971) interpretation of this measure involves assigning quantitative scores to the categories of the condensed ordinal form. For both variables, the category *more* is scored as +1, *same* as 0, and *less* as –1. With knowledge of the independent variable, one makes the ex post linear prediction

$$Y^{*2} = d_{yx}X^{*2}$$

as shown in Figure 3. In other words, if (the condensed ordinal form of) X^{*2} is *more*, then $d_{yx}(+1) = d_{yx}$ is the predicted score; if *same*, then 0 is predicted; and if *less*, then $-d_{yx}$ is predicted. Thus, the measure d_{yx} can also be thought of as analogous to the slope of a linear regression equation. (On re-

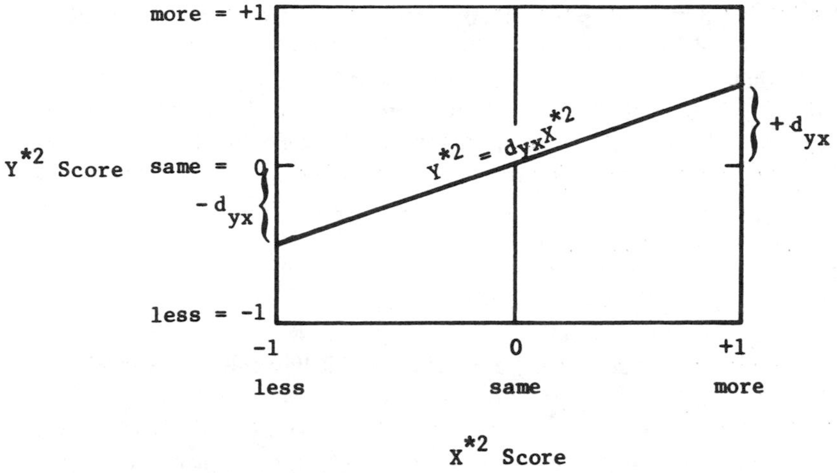

Figure 3: The Linear Model Analogy for the Condensed Form

gression, see the forthcoming paper by Uslaner in this series.) Without knowledge of the independent variable, one always predicts the average score value of the dependent variable, namely zero. Errors are assessed as the square of the difference between observed and predicted values. Thus, for example, if d_{yx} is predicted and *more* (+1) observed, the error is $(1 - d_{yx})^2$; if *same* is observed, $(0 - d_{yx})^2 = d_{yx}^2$; if *less,* $(-1 - d_{yx})^2 = (1 + d_{yx})^2$. Within this scoring, prediction, and error framework, one can now compute r^2, the coefficient of determination. (r^2 is the standard measure of prediction success for linear models of quantitative variables.) It can be shown (but not here) in this instance that $r^2 = \tau_b^2$. Because the +1, 0, −1 scoring system for the condensed form permits this analogy with the linear model, it has received significant attention as a method for analyzing ordinal variables. If the scoring system is accepted, then one can use the whole panopoly of techniques—such as multiple regression, simultaneous equations models, and causal models—that have been developed for quantitative variables.

Before yielding to such a temptation, the researcher should be aware of several limitations. The most fundamental concern relates to the basic analogy. In a linear model for quantitative variables, the assumption is that, if we could remove all the random effects on an observation, the observation's value would lie exactly on the regression line. In the condensed form context, this would mean that when X^{*2} equals *more,* removing the random effects would result in a Y^{*2} value of d_{yx}. But such a value is typically impossible since a pair is always scored +1, 0, or −1. Therefore, it is rather strained to claim a linear, additive relation can exist in the condensed form.

Other limitations relate to using a standard regression program for estimation with *sample* data. One assumption of ordinary least squares regression is that the prediction errors are independent. The radial symmetry property of the condensed form indicates that this assumption is not satisfied. Every time we predict "0" and observe "+1" for example, there must be another pair with a "−1" value. Similarly, another standard assumption is that the amount of variation about the regression line will be the same for all values of the independent variable. It can be shown that this does not hold in general. These limitations imply that standard regression programs will not make the most efficient use of the data. These efficiency limitations become less critical as the sample size grows larger, and can be overcome by a more complex technique known as generalized least squares.

Finally, many testing procedures for linear models assume that the errors have the familiar bell-shaped, unimodal (a bell has only one top), normal distribution. While the procedures are rather robust (one can safely use the tests) under distortions from normality, the distortions are likely to be severe in the case of the condensed form. One can construct condensed form populations where the errors have a bimodal distribution (squared errors of zero occur less frequently than squared errors of one). In addition, the errors are limited to three discrete values, whereas normality pertains to a continuous density.

Mixed Strategies: Mainly as a result of the substantive rather than the statistical limitations of the linear model analogy, we find it useful to relate τ_b^2 to the ∇ framework. To do this we need to extend the prediction framework to include probabilistic or *"mixed"* prediction strategies. (Hildebrand, Laing, and Rosenthal, 1977: ch. 4, contains a more general discussion of mixed strategies.)

To understand mixed strategies, reconsider the predictions underlying d_{yx}. They are *pure* strategy predictions: when the condensed ordinal form of X^{*2} equals *more, always* predict that Y^{*2} is *more,* and so on. Now consider what would happen if, on average, we used the predictions associated with Somers' d_{yx} half the time and those associated with Kim's $d_{y.x}$ half the time. We would have half the observed error rate for d_{yx} plus half the observed error rate for $d_{y.x}$:

$$(.5)[P(\underset{\sim}{D}) + .5P(\underset{\sim}{T}_{Y\bar{X}})] + (.5)[P(\underset{\sim}{D}) + .5P(\underset{\sim}{T}_{\bar{Y}X})]$$

$$= P(\underset{\sim}{D}) + .25P(\underset{\sim}{T}_{Y\bar{X}}) + .25P(\underset{\sim}{T}_{Y\bar{X}})$$

This turns out to be the observed error rate for Kim's symmetric d. Similarly, in using 50-50 randomizations of the predictions underlying d_{yx} and $d_{y.x}$ when they are applied without knowledge of the independent variable, we obtain an expected error rate that also equals that of Kim's symmetric d.

Working through this simple example of mixing predictions illustrates two general facts: (a) we can also evaluate the success of *mixed* strategies as $\nabla = 1 -$ "observed" error/"expected" error and (b) every mixed strategy corresponds to a pure strategy prediction with the same ∇ measure. In this case, the pure strategy ∇-equivalent is the prediction underlying symmetric d.

An alternative and equivalent way of mixing the two asymmetric d predictions is to mix them state-by-state:

If X^{*2} state is	Then with probability	Predict Y^{*2} state is	And Use Error Weights
more	.5	*more*	$\omega_{\underset{\sim}{D}} = 1.0, \omega_{\underset{\sim}{T}_{Y\bar{X}}} = .5, \omega_{\underset{\sim}{C}} = 0.0$
	.5	*more* or *same*	$\omega_{\underset{\sim}{D}} = 1.0, \omega_{\underset{\sim}{T}_{Y\bar{X}}} = \omega_{\underset{\sim}{C}} = 0.0$
same	.5	*more* or *same* or *less*	$\omega_{\underset{\sim}{T}_{Y\bar{X}}} = \omega_{\underset{\sim}{T}_{YX}} = 0.0$
	.5	*same*	$\omega_{\underset{\sim}{T}_{\bar{Y}X}} = .5, \omega_{\underset{\sim}{T}_{YX}} = 0.0$
less	.5	*less*	$\omega_{\underset{\sim}{D}} = 1.0, \omega_{\underset{\sim}{T}_{Y\bar{X}}} = .5, \omega_{\underset{\sim}{C}} = 0.0$
	.5	*less* or *same*	$\omega_{\underset{\sim}{D}} = 1.0, \omega_{\underset{\sim}{T}_{Y\bar{X}}} = \omega_{\underset{\sim}{C}} = 0.0$

State-by-state mixing is the most natural way of stating the predictions that have τ_b^2 as their ∇ measure. In this development we parallel Wilson's (1968) interpretation of τ_b^2. The basic strategy of the τ_b^2 prediction rule is, given an observation pair's condensed ordinal form X^{*2} state, to predict the various Y^{*2} states with the conditional probability in the population in condensed ordinal form: for example, given X^{*2} = *more*, predict Y^{*2} = *more* with the conditional probability observed for this state. From Table 13, the probability that X^{*2} = *more* and Y^{*2} = *more* is $(1/2)P(\underset{\sim}{C})$ while the marginal probability of X^{*2} = *more* is $(1/2)P(\bar{\underset{\sim}{T}}_X)$. Therefore, the appropriate conditional probability is $[(1/2)P(\underset{\sim}{C})] / [(1/2)P(\bar{\underset{\sim}{T}}_X)] = P(\underset{\sim}{C})/P(\bar{\underset{\sim}{T}}_X)$. The other prediction probabilities are similarly computed by dividing Table 13 cell entries by the appropriate column marginals. In evaluating the predictions use the following error weights:

If prediction for pair is that Y^{*2} equals:	then use the following error weights when the pair's observed Y^{*2} state equals:		
	more	*same*	*less*
more	0	1/4	1
same	1/4	0	1/4
less	1	1/4	0

Note that, like the linear model analogy, error weights chosen here are proportional to squared distance in terms of the +1, 0, −1 coding. For example, if *more* is predicted, but *less* is observed, the error weight is always $1 = (1/4)[1-(-1)]^2$ whereas when *more* is predicted but *same* observed, the error weight is always $1/4 = 1/4(1-0)^2$. Also like the linear model analogy, the predictions are determined ex post, reflecting the probabilities observed in the population. Unlike the linear model analogy, however, we always predict a state of the dependent variable that corresponds to one of the possible observed states.

How can we assess error rates for this prediction? Note that the state (*more, more*) occurs with probability $P(\underset{\sim}{C})/2$. On average, following the mixed strategy given above, this event is assigned an error weight of zero for a fraction $P(\underset{\sim}{C})/P(\bar{\underset{\sim}{T}}_X)$ of the times this state is observed; for a fraction $P(\underset{\sim}{T}_{Y\bar{X}})/P(\bar{\underset{\sim}{T}}_X)$, the weight is 1/4; and for a fraction $P(\underset{\sim}{D})/P(\bar{\underset{\sim}{T}}_X)$, the weight is 1.0.

On average, then, the (*more, more*) state is expected to contribute

$$\frac{P(\underset{\sim}{C})}{2}\left[\frac{(1/4)\,P(\underset{\sim}{T}_{Y\bar{X}}) + P(\underset{\sim}{D})}{P(\bar{\underset{\sim}{T}}_X)}\right]$$

to the "observed" error rate. Similarly, by multiplying the appropriate marginal probabilities in Table 13, we find the contribution to the "expected" error rate is

$$\frac{P(\bar{\underset{\sim}{T}}_X)\,P(\bar{\underset{\sim}{T}}_Y)}{4}\left[\frac{(1/4)\,P(\underset{\sim}{T}_{Y\bar{X}}) + P(\underset{\sim}{D})}{P(\bar{\underset{\sim}{T}}_X)}\right]$$

Following analogous procedures, we can also compute the error rate contributions of the other states, make the appropriate summations, and find the ∇ measure, once again, as 1 − "observed" error/"expected" error. Some simplifying algebra then shows that $\nabla = \tau_b^2$. Thus, τ_b^2 is a ∇-measure for the ex post proposition that predicts each state of Y^{*2} in condensed ordinal form with its conditional probability as observed in the population.

Pure Strategy Equivalents: The bracketed term in the error rate contribution for the event (*more, more*) may be interpreted as an error weight for a ∇-equivalent pure strategy prediction. The set of all such error weights is shown in Table 17(a). This underlying pure strategy prediction treats *every* event as an error, but assigns various error weights as determined by the population data.

Having developed a ∇ interpretation of τ_b^2 and knowing that τ_b^2 can also be interpreted as an r^2 statistic suggests another finding, namely, that r^2 for quantitative variables can also be given a ∇ interpretation. We need not enter into that interpretation here. The important point is that the general use of ∇

TABLE 17

Error Weights for the Pure Strategy Prediction Having $\nabla = \tau_b^2$

		X^{*2} more	same	less
Y^{*2}	more	$\frac{P(\underset{\sim}{D}) + \frac{1}{2}P(\underset{\sim}{T}_{Y\bar{X}})}{P(\bar{\underset{\sim}{T}}_{X})}$	$\frac{\frac{1}{2}P(\underset{\sim}{T}_{\bar{Y}X}) + \frac{1}{2}P(\underset{\sim}{T}_{TX})}{P(\underset{\sim}{T}_X)}$	$\frac{P(\underset{\sim}{C}) + \frac{1}{2}P(\underset{\sim}{T}_{Y\bar{X}})}{P(\bar{\underset{\sim}{T}}_X)}$
	same	$\frac{\frac{1}{2}P(\bar{\underset{\sim}{T}})}{P(\bar{\underset{\sim}{T}}_X)}$	$\frac{\frac{1}{2}P(\underset{\sim}{T}_{\bar{Y}X})}{P(\underset{\sim}{T}_X)}$	$\frac{\frac{1}{2}P(\bar{\underset{\sim}{T}})}{P(\bar{\underset{\sim}{T}}_X)}$
	less	$\frac{P(\underset{\sim}{C}) + \frac{1}{2}P(\underset{\sim}{T}_{Y\bar{X}})}{P(\bar{\underset{\sim}{T}}_X)}$	$\frac{\frac{1}{2}P(\underset{\sim}{T}_{\bar{Y}X}) + \frac{1}{2}P(\underset{\sim}{T}_{YX})}{P(\underset{\sim}{T}_X)}$	$\frac{P(\underset{\sim}{D}) + \frac{1}{2}P(\underset{\sim}{T}_{Y\bar{X}})}{P(\bar{\underset{\sim}{T}}_X)}$

measures with ordinal variables presents striking similarities with the standard analysis of quantitative variables.

On to Triples: Spearman's rho_S

Spearman's rho_S is another measure of ordinal association; its relation to the linear model is better known than that of τ_b^2. To illustrate, in both 1975 and 1976 the final standings of the four teams in the Central Division of the National Football League were perfectly ranked—no ties. In 1975, the ranking was (1) Pittsburgh, (2) Cincinnati, (3) Houston, (4) Cleveland. In 1976 (1) Pittsburgh, (2) Cincinnati, (3) Cleveland, (4) Houston. If we were to treat these ranks as quantitative values, then we could compute the ordinary (Pearson) correlation coefficient between the two sets of ranks. In the special case of ranks, this is known as Spearman's (sample) rank correlation coefficient, and the computational procedure becomes very simple:

(1) For each observation, square the difference in ranks on the two variables.

(2) Sum these squares. Call the result SSQ. For the football example,

$$(1-1)^2 + (2-2)^2 + (3-4)^2 + (4-3)^2 = 2 = \text{SSQ}$$

(3) Then, define the rank correlation

$$1 - \frac{6(\text{SSQ})}{N(N^2 - 1)}$$

where N is the sample (or population) size.

In the example, rank correlation = $1 - 6(2)/4(4^2 - 1) = .800$. Continuing to treat the ranks as quantitative information and evaluating prediction error as squared error, the proportionate-reduction-in-error measure analogous to r^2 is the square of this number, or .640. Spearman's rho_S is the population analog of the rank correlation.

Spearman's measure was and perhaps still is used frequently in applied research because, we suspect, it can be readily computed and because it might be interpreted as an analog to quantitative correlation. The interpretive advantage is negated by the disadvantage of making the strong and generally unwarranted assumption that all adjacent categories are separated by equal intervals. The computational advantage has disappeared with the advent of computers and pocket calculators.

Spearman's measure, as suggested by Kruskal (1958), can nonetheless be motivated without recourse to an arbitrary assignment of quantitative values. In the Kruskal approach, rho_S itself, not the square, has a proportionate-reduction-in-error interpretation. Instead of dealing with pairs, one has to deal with triples of observations. As was the case with our initial interpretation of Kendall's tau, consider an infinite, strictly ordered population. Alternatively, permit ties but restrict the domain of the prediction to the subset of triples containing no ties. On a given variable, then, we have only six possible states: I > II > III (which is a shorthand way of saying that the first observation has a greater value—higher rank—than the second, and the second is higher than the third), I > III > II, II > I > III, II > III > I, III > I > II, III > II > I. By symmetry, each of these six states has marginal probability 1/6. A 6x6 table could be needed to represent the relevant cross-tabulation of triples compared on two variables.

Having established the domain of analysis, we turn to the prediction. For the first independent variable state, I > II > III, predict that the dependent variable state of the triple {I > II > III, I > III > II belongs to II > I > III}. For the other five independent variable states, make the analogous predictions by simply making the appropriate interchanges (permutations) of the symbols, I, II, and III. Then it can be shown that $\nabla = rho_S$.

There are several equivalent restatements of this prediction:

(a) At least one of the three members of the pair must be concordant with the other two;

(b) Either the highest of the three observations on the independent variable must also be highest on the dependent, or the lowest must also be lowest;

(c) The highest and lowest independent variable observations must be concordant while the middle observation must be concordant with at least one of the other two observations.

Conceivably, we might move on from the analysis of rho_S to the general analysis of prediction for triples, and might even allow for ties. The basic ∇

framework would still apply. We do not follow such a path, for we agree with Kruskal (1958: 827) that measures for triples like rho_S are "less directly intuitive" than measures for pairs, like τ_b^2, or for single observations, such as the quadrant measure. No other measures for triples are known to us, so we return to pairs.

4. JOINT PREDICTION OF QUANTITATIVE, NOMINAL, AND ORDINAL VARIABLES

We now consider the analysis of predictions using a cross classification of a nominal variable with an ordinal variable, or of a quantitative variable with a qualitative variable.

Quantitative Variables

Many research applications involving ordinal variables include variables using other measurement levels as well. With quantitative variables, one can always elect to treat the variables as ordinal. For example, one can readily compute a condensed ordinal form for a quantitative variable. Positive monotonic transformations (such as multiplying every value by a positive constant or taking the logarithm) of a quantitative variable are order-preserving and, therefore, will not affect its condensed form. On the other hand, any prior decisions about how values are to be grouped into categories will affect the condensed form marginals by affecting the probability of ties. Cell entries for condensed form cross-tabulations also will be affected by decisions about categorization. Hence, all ∇ measures for the condensed form, including the standard measures, will depend on how the Y and X categories are defined—something that is true of ordinal as well as quantitative variables. (As an exercise, combine any two adjacent categories in Table 1 and recompute the condensed form measures.) In effect, choices of categories affect the prediction one is evaluating. Before adopting finer or coarser classifications, therefore, researchers ought to consider the prediction they wish to evaluate.

Nominal Variables and the Extensive Form

Quantitative variables can be analyzed jointly with ordinal variables simply by recognizing that any quantitative variable is also ordinal. But what about simple categorization or nominal variables? To return to the hypothetical population of 100 senators we used earlier, suppose these senators were categorized on region as Northern, Western, and Southern. These three categories have no apparent order. We can, of course, make predictions for single observations as shown earlier in Tables 1-2, 4-9, and 11. For example, the *hypothetical* cross tabulation of a roll call voting scale and region shown in Table 18(a) could be described by the prediction $n \rightsquigarrow$ (*hot, warm,* or *cool*),

TABLE 18
Predicting an Ordinal Variable With a Nominal Variable

(a) Predicting single observations

Roll Call Vote Scale Y by Region

	(n) North	(w) West	(s) South	
hot	.10			.10
warm	.10	.10		.20
cool	.20	.20		.40
cold			.30	.30
	.40	.30	.30	1.00

(N = 100 senators)

Shading indicates unweighted errors for the proposition:
n ↝ (hot, warm, or cool), w ↝ (warm or cool), and s ↝ cold.

(b) Predicting pairs

Region,^{*2} Extensive Form

Scale Y^{*2} Condensed Ordinal Form

	nn	nw	ns	wn	ww	ws	sn	sw	ss	
more	.05	.05	.12	.02	.02	.09				.35
same	.06	.05		.05	.05				.09	.30
less	.05	.02		.05	.02		.12	.09		.35
	.16	.12	.12	.12	.09	.09	.12	.09	.09	1.0

Shading indicates unweighted errors for the proposition:
nw ↝ (more or same), ns ↝ more, wn ↝ (less or same), ws ↝ more,
sn ↝ less, sw ↝ less, and ss ↝ same.

Note: Cells containing no number define events having zero probability.

w ↝ (*warm* or *cool*), & *s* ↝ (*cold*). There are no errors, so $\nabla = 1.0$, while the precision is U = .450.

In order to deal with predictions for pairs, one useful approach is to create the condensed *nominal* form of the region variable by identifying the two states {*same, different*} and proceeding in ways analogous to the foregoing treatment of the condensed ordinal form. The condensed nominal form could be analyzed for the success of a particular prediction using $\nabla_{\mathscr{P}}$.

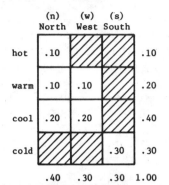

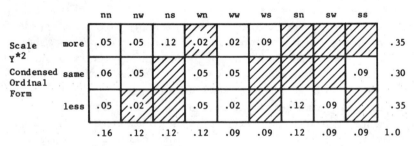

For some research contexts, however, the condensed form destroys essential information. We can preserve this information in the context of prediction of pairs by creating the *extensive* form of a variable. The extensive form of the variable consists of all pairs of variable categories. In the example, the extensive form of the region variable is defined as the $C^2 = 3^2 = 9$ pairs of categories *nn, nw, ns, wn, ww, ws, sn, sw,* and *ss*. The marginal probability of any pair is simply the product of the marginals for the two categories entering the pair. For example, P(*ns*) = P(*sn*) = P(*n*)P(*s*) = .4(.3) = .12.

Analysts then might proceed to look at the relation between this *extensive form* of the region variable and the *condensed ordinal form* of the roll call scale. The relevant probabilities are shown in Table 18(b). For example, the probability of (*same, nn*) is found simply by summing up the squares of the cell probabilities in the *n* column of Table 18(a):

$$P(\textit{same}, \textit{nn}) = (.1)^2 + (.1)^2 + (.2)^2 + (.0)^2 = .06$$

Paralleling analysis of the condensed ordinal form, we can now use symmetry to obtain the other probabilities in the *nn* column in Table 18(b):

$$P(\textit{more}, \textit{nn}) = P(\textit{less}, \textit{nn}) = (1/2)\,[P(\textit{nn}) - P(\textit{same}, \textit{nn})]$$

$$= (1/2)(.16 - .06) = .05$$

Similarly, the probability (*same,nw*) is found by multiplying, row-by-row, the probabilities in column *n* and column *w* of Table 18(a) and summing:

$$P(\textit{same}, \textit{nw}) = (.1)(.0) + (.1)(.1) + (.2)(.2) + (.0)(.0) = .05$$

The probability of (*more,nw*) can be computed by taking each entry in column *n* and multiplying it by the sum of all entries in column *w* that have lower roll call scores, and then summing the resulting products:

$$P(\textit{more}, \textit{nw}) = .1(.1 + .2 + .0) + .1(.2 + .0) + 2(.0) = .05$$

To obtain the final entry in the *nw* column,

$$P(\textit{less}, \textit{nw}) = P(\textit{nw}) - P(\textit{more}, \textit{nw}) - P(\textit{same}, \textit{nw}) = .02$$

Note that symmetry can now be used to obtain the entries of the *wn* column from the *nw* column.

Consider the prediction that both northern and western senators will have higher roll call scores than southerners, and that northerners will have scores at least as high as westerners. Moreover, within regions, southerners are expected to have identical scores whereas no prediction is made for pairs of northerners or pairs of western senators. This prediction, shown in Table 18(b), has a ∇ value of .905 and U = .420.

Now consider the alternative prediction with weighted errors shown in Table 19(a). We can clearly get an equivalent prediction and equal ∇ value by

TABLE 19
The Equivalent Extensive Form Representation of a Condensed Form Proposition

(a) The extensive form representation

Region,*2 Extensive Form

Roll Call Scale,*2 Condensed Form		nn	nw	ns	wn	ww	ws	sn	sw	ss
	more				1			1	1	
	same		1/2	1/2	1/2		1/2	1/2	1/2	
	less		1	1			1			

(b) A condensed form representation

Region*2

Roll Call Scale,*2 Condensed Form		(nw,ns,ws) "more"	(nn,ww,ss) same	(wn,sn,sw) "less"
	more			1
	same	1/2		1/2
	less	1		

Note: Both tables show error weights underlying Somers' d_{yx}.

combining columns with identical error weights. As shown in Table 19(b), let *"more"* be the combination of *nw, ns,* and *ws, same* combine *nn, ww,* and *ss,* and *"less"* combine *wn, sn,* and *sw*. From inspection of Table 19(b), we see that the combination reflects a scaling of the three categories in the order n, w, s and that the prediction of Table 19(a) is equivalent to that underlying Somers' d_{yx}, except, of course, that d_{yx} is defined for two ordinal variables. (The scaling, suggested by inspection of Table 18(a), may be relevant only to that cross-tabulation. On some other issue, the three nominal categories could well have a different order. Note further that the prediction of Table 18(b) cannot be represented in this condensed form.)

Treating the region as a set of ordered categories shows that we can represent ordinal as well as nominal variables in extensive form. While for some purposes, an extensive form analysis of two ordinal variables might be preferable to a condensed form analysis, this paper has emphasized the condensed form because of its prominence in the literature. In any event, *every condensed form prediction has an equivalent representation in extensive form.*

When the hypothetical data of Table 18(a) are analyzed with the categories of Table 19(b), the values of various measures are

	∇	U^c
gamma	.857	.280
d_{yx}	.727	.330
$d_{y.x}$	.686	.350
d	.706	.340
e	.600	.400

These results show that the prediction represented in Table 18(b), for which we found ∇ = .905 and U = .420, dominates the predictions underlying the conventional measures.

Another equivalence theorem states that *every prediction for single observations can be represented as an equivalent prediction for pairs in extensive form* (Hildebrand, Laing and Rosenthal, 1977: appendix 5.1). We can use this theorem with the $\nabla_{\mathcal{P}}$ and U^c measures to conclude that the prediction represented in Table 18(b) is, in turn, dominated by the proposition which identifies the error events shaded in Table 18(a) since this latter proposition has both a larger ∇ (1.0 vs. .905) and U^c (.450 vs. .420).

Thus, to conclude this section, we find that the extensive form for pairs provides a framework for the comparative analysis of predictions involving different levels of measurement and relating either pairs or single observations.

5. MULTIVARIATE ANALYSIS

The limits of this paper permit only a brief glance at multivariate analysis. Whereas the basic methods for multivariate analysis of quantitative variables using linear models have been around for half a century, multivariate methods for ordinal variables are only beginning to be worked out. For one thing, multivariate methods for ordinal data should provide "partial" measures that assess the relation between two variables when the effects of one or more other variables are controlled. Only a few partial measures of ordinal association have been provided earlier in the literature. These are often inappropriate for many research problems. The multivariate methods should be designed to evaluate specific predictions.

In this section we suggest an approach to the evaluation of multivariate predictions with ordinal data. The methods described in this section can be used in general to design ∇ measures of overall and partial prediction success for evaluating multivariate predictions. Fortunately, the basic principles of the multivariate ∇ methods in general can be illustrated with a three-variable problem. These principles apply whether single observations or pairs are the focus of interest. In working out the details of an example, we have chosen to look at pair prediction since pairs have occupied most of the literature on ordinal association. A general treatment of the ∇ methods for multivariate prediction analysis of qualitative variables is offered in Hildebrand, Laing, and Rosenthal (1977: ch. 7).

Let us return to the bureaucrat example, adding a third (hypothetical) variable. Let this be whether the bureaucrat believes corporate taxes should be *raised, unchanged,* or *lowered*. We are interested in using the previous variables—party affiliation and support for social services—to predict attitudes toward taxes. There are important causal problems: perhaps views on taxes also influence both party affiliation and support for social services. In this paper, however, we focus only on prediction, leaving interpretations based on beliefs about causation to the judgment of the investigator.

Setting Up the Trivariate Condensed Form

The easiest way to handle a multivariate problem is to transform it into an equivalent bivariate problem. To do this, consider the 5 x 3 = 15 ways of pairing each of the first independent variable (social services) states with a state of the other independent variable (affiliation). The categories of this composite independent variable are *(left,Dem)*, *(left,Ind)*, *(left,Rep)*, *(left-center,Dem)*, *(left-center,Ind)*, . . . , *(right,Rep)*. The joint distribution of 31 bureaucrats on these 15 categories with the three categories of the dependent variable is shown in the 3 x 15 arrangement of Table 20(a). While the joint distribution is hypothetical, note that the marginals of the composite independent variable are just the cell entries from Table 1.

Similarly, the *condensed ordinal forms* of the two independent variables can be combined into a composite variable with the nine states *(more,more)*, *(more,same)*, *(more,less)*, *(same,more)*, . . . , *(less,less)*. The joint distribution of the 961 pairs of bureaucrats on these nine categories and the three condensed form categories of the dependent variable is shown in Table 20(b). The marginal numbers of cases on the composite independent variable are equal to the cell entries of Table 3.

The cell entries in Table 20(b) can be computed from those in Table 20(a) in a manner similar to those used to compute Tables 3 and 18(b). For example, the number of pairs that are the *same* on *all three* variables is found by

TABLE 20
Three-Way Tabulation of Corporate Tax Attitudes versus Party Affiliation and Social Services Support

(a) Single observations

	Social Services	Left			Left-center			Center			Right-center			Right			
	Affiliation	Dem	Ind	Rep	Dem	Ind	Rep	Dem	Ind	Rep	Dem	Ind	Rep	Dem	Ind	Rep	
Corporate Tax	Raised	12	2														14
	Unchanged		1	1	1	2	1		3	3							12
	Lowered						1			1		1	1			1	5
		12	3	1	1	2	2	0	3	4	0	1	1	0	0	1	31 bureaucrats

(b) Condensed ordinal form for observation pairs

	Social Services *2	more			same			less			
	Affiliation *2	more	same	less	more	same	less	more	same	less	
Corporate Tax *2	more	204	43	7	32	6		3	3		298
	same	17	24	12	40	179	40	12	24	17	365
	less		3	3		6	32	7	43	204	298
		221	70	22	72	191	72	22	70	221	961 pairs

Note: Blank cells contain zero cases.

squaring each cell entry in Table 20(a) and summing. This sum equals 179. Subtracting from 191, the marginal total of *same-same* cases on the composite independent variable, and (by symmetry) dividing by two, yields six pairs in both the (*more, same, same*) and (*less, same, same*) cells.

To find the number of pairs that are in the upper left-hand cell (*more, more, more*) begin by noting that the 12 (*raised, left, Dem*) bureaucrats exhibit the (*more, more, more*) relation with all bureaucrats who are neither *raised* nor *left* nor *Dem*. Inspection of the table shows there are 2 + 1 + 1 + 3 + 3 + 1 + 1 + 1 + 1 = 14 such bureaucrats. Therefore, (*raised, left, Dem*) contributes 12 x 14 = 168 relevant pairs. Similarly, the two (*raised, left, Ind*) observations exhibit the desired relation with all observations that are *Rep* but neither *raised* nor *left*. There are 1 + 1 + 3 + 1 + 1 + 1 = 8 such observations, so (*raised, left, Ind*) contributes 2 x 8 = 16 relevant pairs. Continuing in this way to process all cells of Table 20(a), we find that the single (*unchanged, left, Ind*) bureaucrat is (*more, more, more*) with all bureaucrats who are *lowered* and *Rep* but not *left*. The 1 + 1 + 1 + 1 = 4 such bureaucrats lead to a contribution of four pairs. The other non-zero contributions are 1 + 1 + 1 + 1 = 4 for (*unchanged, left-center, Dem*), 2 x (1 + 1 + 1) = 6 for (*unchanged, left-center, Ind*), and 3 x (1 + 1) = 6 for (*unchanged, center, Ind*). Finally, summing all contributions shows 168 + 16 + 4 + 4 + 6 + 6 = 204 (*more, more, more*) pairs. Analogous computations and the use of symmetry considerations allow all the entries in the Table 20(b) to be computed from those in Table 20(a).

Trivariate Representation of Bivariate Predictions: As a prelude to multivariate analysis, note first that any bivariate prediction for the condensed form can be represented in terms of Table 20(b). Consider the bivariate proposition $\mathcal{A}$ which contains the d_{yx} predictions of each bureaucrat's attitude toward corporate tax on the basis of his party *a*ffiliation. Table 21(a) shows the correct set of error weights for d_{yx}. The error weights for *more* on affiliation, for example, appear in *every column* that is *more* on affiliation. Table 21(b) shows the error weights for the proposition $\mathcal{S}$, representing the d_{yx} predictions of corporate tax attitudes from support for social services. We could compute the d_{yx} measures directly from Table 20(b). It is easier, especially since we have the short-hand formula $[P(\underset{\sim}{C}) - P(\underset{\sim}{D})]/P(\overline{\underset{\sim}{T}}_X)$ for d_{yx}, to collapse Table 20(b) into Tables 22(a) and (b). Applying this formula and recalling that $U_{d_{yx}} = \frac{1}{2} P(\overline{\underset{\sim}{T}}_X)$ yields

$$\nabla_{\mathcal{A}} = d_{yx} = [478/961 - 14/961]/[630/961] = .737, \quad U_{\mathcal{A}} = .328$$

$$\nabla_{\mathcal{S}} = d_{yx} = [508/961 - 12/961]/[626/961] = .792, \quad U_{\mathcal{S}} = .326$$

TABLE 21
The Trivariate Representation of a Bivariate Prediction

(a) Party affiliation predicting corporate tax attitudes

	Social Services *2	more			same			less		
	Affiliation *2	more	same	less	more	same	less	more	same	less
Corporate Tax Attitude *2	more			1			1			1
	same	1/2		1/2	1/2		1/2	1/2		1/2
	less	1			1			1		

(b) Support for social services as predictor of corporate tax attitudes

	Social Services *2	more			same			less		
	Affiliation *2	more	same	less	more	same	less	more	same	less
Corporate Tax Attitude *2	more							1	1	1
	same	1/2	1/2	1/2				1/2	1/2	1/2
	less	1	1	1						

Note: Error weights are those for predictions underlying Somers' d_{yx}.

Neither of these propositions dominates the other. One way to take both dimensions (precision and prediction success) into account is to compare the two propositions in terms of their reduction (not proportionate) in error:

$$\text{expected error rate} - \text{observed error rate} = U_{\wp}\nabla_{\wp}$$

In this case $U_{\mathcal{S}}\nabla_{\mathcal{S}} = .258 > U_A\nabla_A = .241$. Assume a researcher had in fact used $\mathcal{S}$ as the bivariate model and was interested in how the affiliation variable might be introduced into the prediction.

Introducing a Third Variable: The following asymmetric treatment of the variables is just one of many ways in which the third variable, affiliation,

TABLE 22

Bivariate Tabulations of Condensed Forms

(a) Corporate tax attitude versus party affiliation

		Party Affiliation*2			
		more	same	less	
Corporate Tax*2	more	239	52	7	298
	same	69	227	69	365
	less	7	52	239	298
		315	331	315	961 pairs

(b) Corporate tax versus social services attitudes

		Social Services*2			
		more	same	less	
Corporate Tax*2	more	254	38	6	298
	same	53	259	53	365
	less	6	38	254	298
		313	335	313	961 pairs

might affect the bivariate prediction. First, consider pairs that are tied (*same*) on social services. For these pairs, use the affiliation variable as a tiebreaker by imposing the $\mathscr{a}$ predictions. Second, consider pairs that are concordant on the independent variables—the extreme columns of Table 20(b). Here one willing to treat ties as serious errors could make a strong prediction of concordance on the dependent variable and assign an error weight of one rather than the 1/2 shown in the cells in the *same* row and both the (*more,more*) and (*less,less*) columns. Otherwise, the social services prediction is maintained. The complete trivariate prediction is illustrated in Table 23.

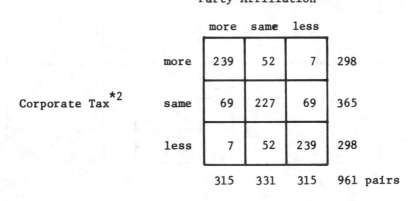

TABLE 23
Set of Trivariate Error Weights After Modifying the Bivariate Proposition

	Social Services*2	more			same			less		
	Affiliation*2	more	same	less	more	same	less	more	same	less
Corporate Tax*2	more						1	1	1	1
	same	1	1/2	1/2	1/2		1/2	1/2	1/2	1
	less	1	1	1	1					

Multiple ∇

The proportion of the total population that constitutes weighted observed errors for this trivariate prediction equals

$$\frac{2[17 + (.5)24 + (.5)12 + (.5)40 + 0 + 3 + 3 + 0]}{961} = \frac{122}{961} = .127$$

(The data are found in Table 20(b) and the error weights in Table 23. Errors from the left-hand side of Table 20(b) are entered in the sum, which then can be multiplied by 2 because of symmetry.)

The proportion of the pairs constituting weighted "expected" error is:

$$\frac{2\{365[221 + (.5)70 + (.5)22 + .5(72)] + 298[221 + 70 + 22 + 72]\}}{961^2}$$

$$= \frac{450{,}650}{923{,}521} = .488$$

Combining these results, we find

$$\text{multiple } \nabla = 1 - \frac{\text{trivariate prediction error observed}}{\text{trivariate prediction error expected}}$$

$$= 1 - \frac{.127}{.488} = .740$$

$$U = .488$$

Consequently, the trivariate prediction achieves a substantial increase in precision (.49 vs. .33) when compared to either bivariate proposition while its prediction success (∇) value is comparable to the bivariate measures (.74 vs. .72 for $\mathcal{A}$ and .79 for $\mathcal{S}$). Accordingly, the trivariate proposition attains a reduction in error of $U\nabla$ = .361, higher than either bivariate proposition.

Partial ∇

We next develop a measure for evaluating the contribution of one independent variable to the multivariate proposition's success when the effects of the other independent variable(s) are taken into account. In the example, we will define a partial del to measure that part of the trivariate proposition's success that can be attributed solely to the affiliation variable when the social services variable is held constant.

Let us create three subpopulations, so that all pairs within a subpopulation have the same state on the condensed ordinal form of the social services variable: *more, same,* or *less*. Within each of these subpopulations the social services variable is constant. One way to assess the partial contribution of the affiliation variable is to determine how well the trivariate proposition predicts in each of those three subpopulations.

Subpopulation Partial ∇'s: Recall that within the subpopulation of pairs that are tied (*same*) on social services, the trivariate prediction applies the d_{yx} predictions for affiliation. As a measure of the partial prediction success contributed by affiliation in the *same* social services subpopulation, compute d_{yx} for *only the 335 pairs in this subpopulation*. From Table 20(b), we have:

$$\textit{same} \text{ subpopulation partial } \nabla = d_{yx} = (64/335 - 0/335)/(144/335)$$
$$= .444$$

Thus, using affiliation as a tiebreaker for social services was only moderately successful. For future use, note that the weighted errors for the d_{yx} predictions in the social services^{*2} = *same* subpoluation are:

$$\text{“observed”} = 2\,[(.5)40 + 0] = 40$$
$$\text{“expected”} = [2(72)/335]\;[(.5)259 + 38] = 72$$

Thus, *same* subpopulation

$$\text{Partial } \nabla = 1 - \frac{\text{observed errors for the trivariate proposition, given the affiliation state in } \textit{same} \text{ subpopulation}}{\text{expected errors for the trivariate proposition, given the } \textit{same} \text{ subpopulation but not the affiliation state}}$$

Similarly, we can see how the trivariate prediction does within the 313 pairs of the subpopulation in which social services = *more* by computing ∇ for the trivariate proposition within this subpopulation. The weighted errors (refer to Table 23 for the weights) are

$$\text{“observed”} = [17 + (.5)24 + (.5)12 + 0 + 3 + 3] = 41$$

$$\text{“expected”} = \frac{53}{313} \text{ x } [221 + (.5)70 + (.5)22] + \frac{6}{313} \text{ x } [221 + 70 + 22] = 51.21$$

so that the *more* subpopulation partial ∇ = 1 – 41/51.21 = .199. By symmetry, this is also the partial ∇ for the social services = *less* subpopulation.

Note that this partial has a low, but positive value. Comparing the error weights shown in Tables 21(b) and 23, we see that, in the *more* subpopulation, the trivariate prediction modifies *S* only by adding an additional .5 error weight to the cell in the *same* row and (*more, more*) column. The partial is low despite the fact that in this cell the component (partial) ∇ value is

$$1 - \frac{17/313}{(221/313)\,(53/313)} = .546$$

However, for the added weight, the subpopulation precision component is only $(.5)221 \text{ x } 53/313^2 = .060$. In contrast, the bivariate, undifferentiated predictions of $\mathscr{S}$ in this subpopulation have a subpopulation ∇ of zero but a precision of 6/313 + (.5)53/313 = .104. The complete subpopulation ∇ (subpopulation partial) can be expressed as a weighted average of these two components:

$$\textit{more} \text{ subpopulation partial } \nabla = \frac{1}{.060 + .104} [.060(.546) + .104(0)] = .199$$

Thus, even though the trivariate prediction adds to the error weight of a cell with a moderately large ∇ value, the partial contribution to prediction success remains very modest because, over the entire subpopulation, the trivariate prediction is largely undifferentiated.

The Overall Partial ∇*:* Reviewing the results for the three subpopulations on social services, we can see that the primary contribution of the affiliation variable to the trivariate proposition's success is within the *same* subpopulation. Having the results for these three subpopulations is useful. It would also be helpful to have a single, partial measure for the contribution of affiliation to the trivariate prediction that takes all three subpopulations into account while controlling for the social services variable. To achieve this, we again take the standard approach: add up the observed errors for each subpopulation, add up the expected errors, and compute a ∇ measure. We have

$$\text{"observed"} = 41 + 40 + 41 = 122$$

$$\text{"expected"} = 51.21 + 72 + 51.21 = 174.4$$

partial ∇, controlling support for social services

$$= 1 - \frac{122}{174.4} = .301$$

$$= 1 - \frac{\text{trivariate prediction errors knowing condensed form states of both affiliation and social services}}{\text{trivariate prediction errors knowing condensed form state of social services only}}$$

(As an exercise, continue to use the error weights shown in Table 23 but compute the partial controlling for affiliation.)

As before, we can express the overall partial as a weighted average of the subpopulation partials where the weights are precision measures. Note that the U^c value for the partial in the social services = *same* subpopulation is

U^c = (precision of *same* subpopulation partial) x (proportion of pairs for which social services = *same*)

$= (72/335)\,(335/961) = 72/961$

Each of the other two components have $U^c = 51.21/961$. Then the overall partial ∇ is a weighted average of the three subpopulation partials, each weighted by its contribution to the overall expected error rate for the trivariate proposition. Thus, the partial ∇, controlling for social services

$$= \frac{1}{(51.21 + 72 + 51.21)/961} [(51.21/961)(.199) + (72/961)(.444) + (51.21/961)(.199)]$$

$$= .301$$

We emphasize that the subpopulation partials that can be averaged to form an overall partial are distinct from subpopulation component trivariate ∇ values that could be averaged to find multiple ∇. The observed errors are the same for both subpopulation quantities. But the expected errors for the subpopulation partial are based on marginal totals for the subpopulation only, whereas the expected errors for the components of the multiple del are based on the marginals for the whole population. For example, the "expected" errors for the social services = *more* component of the multiple would be

$$\frac{365}{961}\,[221 + (.5)70 + (.5)22] \;+\; \frac{298}{961}\,[221 + 70 + 22] = 198.47$$

rather than the 51.21 we found for the subpopulation partial.

The "expected" error rate used in the partial is the result of applying the trivariate theory with knowledge of the social services state but not the affiliation state. The "observed" errors are those that result when one has knowledge of both independent variables. Consequently, the partial assesses the proportionate-reduction-in-error when one applies the trivariate theory with knowledge of both variables rather than with knowledge of only one variable (social services in the example). In contrast, the multiple ∇ measures the proportionate-reduction-in-error when one predicts with knowledge of both as against predicting with knowledge of neither.

In classical multivariate analysis using a linear model there is the following result:

$$\frac{\text{errors of } \textit{tri}\text{variate prediction knowing BOTH independent variables}}{\text{errors of } \textit{tri}\text{variate prediction knowing NEITHER independent variable}}$$

$$= \left[\frac{\text{errors of } \textit{tri}\text{variate prediction knowing BOTH independent variables}}{\text{errors of } \textit{tri}\text{variate prediction knowing just ONE (social services) independent variable}}\right]$$

$$\times \left[\frac{\text{errors of } \textit{bi}\text{variate prediction } S \text{ knowing the independent variable (social services)}}{\text{errors of } \textit{bi}\text{variate prediction } S \textit{ without} \text{ knowing the independent variable (social services)}}\right]$$

In terms of the del measures, the analogous "accounting" expression would be

$$(1 - \text{multiple } \nabla) = (1 - \text{partial } \nabla)\,(1 - \text{bivariate } \nabla)$$

But, using the results from the example,

$$(1 - .740) = .260 \neq .145 = (1 - .301)\,(1 - .792)$$

The classical result for linear models provides a direct and convenient basis for error accounting. The result requires not only the assumption of squared error but also the assumption that variables enter a model by being added on. For example, when the bivariate prediction is, say, $Y = 1.5X$, the trivariate prediction must be something like $Y = .8X + .9Z$, the Z term being added to the prediction equation. In such cases, the classical result leads to the well-known partial measure. On the other hand, although non-additive equations such as Y = XZ frequently appear in research, no one computes a partial measure for the contribution of Z in such cases—although the prediction analysis approach could be used for this purpose.

When the "accounting" equation fails to hold, as in our example, one has to take prediction "shifts" into account. These shifts relate to the changing form of the prediction when one goes from a bivariate to a trivariate prediction as against the additional information value of the variables summarized in the partial (see Hildebrand, Laing, and Rosenthal, 1977: ch. 7). Much useful analysis can be done using just multiple and partial dels, although complete mastery of multivariate analysis requires understanding of the shifts.

Davis' Partial gamma: We now relate the foregoing discussion to a special case which has been prominent in the literature. Consider the subpopulation shown in Table 24, where ties on the dependent variable have been deleted. As shown in an earlier section, we can interpret the bivariate gamma between social services and corporate tax as being based on the prediction identifying the horizontally shaded cells as error events. This gamma can be readily computed from Table 22 (b) as

$$\text{gamma} = (508 - 12)/(508 + 12) = .954$$

Davis' (1967) partial gamma is simply the bivariate gamma measure on the relation between two variables as applied only to the subpopulation of pairs that are tied (*same*) on the control variable. Thus, in the example, Davis'

TABLE 24
Trivariate Gamma Analysis

	Social Services *2	more			same			less			
	Affiliation *2	more	same	less	more	same	less	more	same	less	
Corporate Tax *2	more	204	43	7	32	6		3	3		298
	less		3	3		6	32	7	43	204	298
		204	46	10	32	12	32	10	46	204	596 pairs

Horizontally-shaded cells are error events underlying bivariate gamma for Social Services and Corporate Tax Attitudes.

Vertically-shaded cells are error events for Davis' partial gamma.

All shaded cells are error events for "trivariate gamma."

partial gamma equals the simple gamma in the social services = *same* subpopulation:

$$\text{Davis' partial gamma} = (64 - 0)/(64 + 0) = 1.000$$

This is fine as a subpopulation partial, but consider the precision of the prediction

$$U^c = .5(64/961) = .033$$

The numerical value is not only small in this example; it will always tend to be small because of the exclusion of ties and because the scope of the prediction extends to only one of the three subpopulations on social services.[3] If a single number is to be used as *the* "partial gamma," we think it ought to be an overall partial. What appears to be the natural trivariate prediction within the gamma framework is to retain the bivariate gamma predictions within the *more* and *less* subpopulations and to use the Davis tiebreaker prediction in the *same* subpopulation. In this case, the *more* and *less* subpopulation partials always will be zero. Affiliation does not differentiate predictions in these subpopulations and cannot contribute to error reduction there.

The resulting composite prediction identifies all shaded cells in Table 24 as error events. For multiple ∇,

$$\text{"observed errors"} = 2(3 + 3 + 0) = 12$$

$$\text{"expected errors"} = 2\left(\frac{298}{596}\right)(260 + 3) = 292$$

$$\text{multiple } \nabla = 1 - 12/292 = .959, \quad U^c = .304$$

For partial ∇, controlling for social services, we have,

$$\text{"observed errors"} = 2(3 + 3 + 0) = 12$$

$$\text{"expected errors"} = 2(6) + 2(32/76)(38) = 44$$

$$\text{partial } \nabla = 1 - 12/44 = .727, \quad U^c = .046$$

The Davis predictions make no error in the social services = *same* subpopulation, but there are still some errors left in the other subpopulations, reducing partial ∇ to .727 for the entire domain of the trivariate prediction.

Somers (1964, 1968, 1970, 1974) has developed various partial measures in the τ_b^2 and d_{yx} framework. (Again, as was shown earlier for the bivariate case, there is an analogy to the linear model; our earlier criticisms of this analogy obviously extend to multivariate analysis.) Like the Davis partial, Somers' work can be explicated via ∇, but the technical developments run beyond the scope of this paper. In any event, we suggest that researchers develop directly the particular bivariate and trivariate condensed form error weights that are appropriate to their research problems. This custom-designing strategy is better than searching the literature in the hope of finding a traditional measure that is appropriate.

6. COMPUTING AND STATISTICAL INFERENCE

The examples considered in the last section have been used to illustrate the basic mechanics of multivariate prediction analysis of ordinal variables. This discussion, like the bivariate treatment, always referred to populations. In research, the data almost always are a sample from a larger population. In the most common case, namely simple random sampling, the natural way to get a single number that is an *estimate* of the true population value of any ∇ is simply to compute the sample analog. Just plug in the number of sample cases or pairs where we used, for example, the population number of bureaucrats or pairs of bureaucrats. Alternatively, use sample proportions in place of population probabilities. (Computation is relatively simple, especially when the prediction is for single observations.) Sum the weighted observed errors. Compute the products needed to get the weighted "expected" errors and sum those. Divide the "observed" by the "expected" error rate, and subtract from one. Each of the calculations in this paper was done in a few minutes with a pocket calculator.

Computer Programs

Many of the standard measures for ordinal variables can be calculated using "canned" computer programs. For example, the SPSS program can be used to cross-classify qualitative data and to compute values of such bivariate measures as gamma, Kendall's τ_b^2, and the Somers' measures. Two free-standing programs in FORTRAN IV are available from the authors for computing $\nabla_{\wp}$ and various associated test statistics for (1) bivariate and (2) multivariate prediction analysis of qualitative data. These programs require as input the cross-classified data of interest, and the specific prediction and set of error weights to be evaluated. In addition, a bivariate $\nabla_{\wp}$ program which can be added to the Control Data Corporation version of SPSS as a subroutine is now available.[4] Programs can be obtained from the authors at the University of Pennsylvania.

Statistical Inference

With a sample, though, an estimate of ∇ is not enough. One also wants to know something about the variability of that estimate. For example, one often wants to test the hypothesis that the true value of ∇ is greater than zero. Or one may want to compute a *confidence interval* that gives a range of values that can be expected to include the true value of ∇ in, say, about 95 of every 100 independent samples. An introduction to methods for statistical inference is covered in the paper by Henkel (1976) in this series. The specific methods of statistical inference for prediction analyses based on the various $\nabla_{\mathscr{P}}$ measures are given in Hildebrand, Laing, and Rosenthal (1977: Ch. 6 and 7). Consequently, we will not get into inference in this introductory paper, except for two brief comments.

First, especially with a priori predictions, the conventional wisdom of having at least five cases in each cell of a cross-tabulation does not hold. With ∇ it is the set of *all* error cells as a *whole* that matters. As long as the marginals are not too badly skewed, one should not be deterred from the prediction analysis of large tables, even if the sample has only 25 to 100 cases. (The $\nabla_{\mathscr{P}}$ programs described earlier automatically print out a warning when the sample is too small to rely on the test statistics for the prediction under consideration.)

Second, with appropriate specification of the error weights, the ∇ program will produce any of the conventional measures discussed in this paper and, therefore, will also produce test statistics and confidence intervals for these measures, something that frequently is not supplied by the conventional canned programs.

Conclusion

This paper has presented an overview of prediction analysis methods for ordinal variables. A great deal of the paper was devoted to developing and interpreting some standard measures of ordinal association. We did not cover everything. But we aimed at what is most widely used in social science.

Because most of these measures are based on the condensed form for ordinal comparisons of observation pairs, prediction for pairs received more attention here than prediction for single observations. The emphasis of this paper is intended to be useful in reading past analyses of social science data. Hopefully, readers of this paper who encounter gamma, tau, and d measures in the literature will understand what is being measured and thereby understand the strengths and limitations of the measures and their relevance to the substantive problems of the investigation.

Despite the emphasis of past literature on a series of special measures for observation pairs, we by no means advocate continuing this emphasis in future research. We believe instead that future research should focus more on the prediction of individual observations than on paired comparisons. Above all, we urge researchers to specify predictions and related error weights that are relevant to their research purposes rather than somewhat blindly selecting, say, gamma because it is "accepted" and known to a certain audience.

We have provided some guidance to researchers interested in simple verbal propositions of "the *more* X, the *more* Y" variety. A sensitivity analysis approach was offered as an alternative to selecting a fixed measure. The real challenge to researchers, however, is to move beyond the analysis of loosely specified verbal theory relating two or three variables to the analysis of more precisely specified scientific models. When the task of model building is accomplished, the researcher should then apply methods of data analysis that are designed to evaluate the model's specific predictions.

NOTES

1. The last line holds because the 50-50 splits imply $P_{y\bar{x}} = P_{\bar{y}x}$. (Prove as an exercise.)

2. Note that $P(\underset{\sim}{T}_{YX})$ contains (but is not restricted to) the probability of self-ties. In finite populations, this probability of a self-tie equals 1/N. For some purposes, one may wish to exclude self-ties from analysis. In infinite populations the problem does not arise since the limiting value of 1/N is zero.

3. The situation gets even worse, if, as Davis (1967) suggests, we attempt to control for several variables by looking only at cases that are tied on *all* the control variables.

4. For this we are grateful for the efforts of Deborah Lurie, Temple University, and Professor Richard Heiberger, University of Pennsylvania.

REFERENCES

ABERBACH, J. D. and B. A. ROCKMAN (1976) "Clashing beliefs within the executive branch: the Nixon bureaucracy." Amer. Pol. Sci. Rev. 70: 456-468.

BLALOCK, H. M., Jr. (1960) Social Statistics. New York: McGraw-Hill.

COHEN, J. (1968) "Weighted kappa: nominal scale agreement with provision for scaled disagreement or partial credit." Psych. Bull. 70: 213-220.

--- (1960) "A coefficient of agreement for nominal scales." Educational and Psychological Measurement 20: 37-46.

DAVIS, J. A. (1967) "A partial coefficient for Goodman and Kruskal's gamma." J. of Amer. Stat. Assn. 62: 184-193.

DEUCHLER, G. (1914) "Über die Methoden der Korrelationsrechnung in der Pädagogik und Psychologie." Zeitschrift für Pädagogische Psychologie und Experimentelle Pädagogik 15: 114-131, 145-159, 229-242. Cited by Goodman and Kruskal (1959).

GOODMAN, L. A. and W. H. KRUSKAL (1959) "Measures of association for cross-classifications, II: further discussions and references." J. of Amer. Stat. Assn. 54: 123-163.

--- (1954) "Measures of association for cross-classifications." J. of Amer. Stat. Assn. 49: 732-764.

HAWKES, R. K. (1971) "The multivariate analysis of ordinal measures." Amer. J. of Sociology 76: 908-926.

HENKEL, R. (1976) Tests of Significance. Sage University Papers on Quantitative Applications in the Social Sciences, 07-004. Beverly Hills and London: Sage Pub.

HILDEBRAND, D. K., J. D. LAING, and H. ROSENTHAL (1977) Prediction Analysis of Cross Classifications. New York: Wiley.

--- (1976) "Prediction analysis in political research." Amer. Pol. Sci. Rev. 70: 509-535.

--- (1975) "A prediction logic approach to causal models of qualitative variates," pp. 146-175 in D. R. Heise (ed.) Sociological Methodology (1975) San Francisco: Jossey-Bass.

--- (1974a) "Prediction logic: a method for empirical evaluation of formal theory." J. of Math. Sociology 3: 163-185.

--- (1974b) "Prediction logic and quasi-independence in empirical evaluation of formal theory." J. of Math. Sociology 3: 197-209.

KENDALL, M. G. (1962) Rank Correlation Methods (3rd ed.) London: Charles Griffin.

KIM, J. (1971) "Predictive measures of ordinal association." Amer. J. of Sociology 76: 891-907.

KRUSKAL, W. H. (1958) "Ordinal measures of association." J. of Amer. Stat. Assn. 53: 814-861.

NEWELL, A. and H. A. SIMON (1972) Human Problem Solving. Englewood Cliffs, N.J.: Prentice-Hall.

REYNOLDS, H. T. (1977) Analysis of Nominal Data. Sage University Papers on Quantitative Applications in the Social Sciences, 07-007. Beverly Hills and London: Sage Pub.

SOMERS, R. H. (1974) "Analysis of partial rank correlation measures based on the product-moment model: part one." Social Forces 53: 229-246.

--- (1970) "A partitioning of ordinal information in a three-way cross-classification." Multivariate Behavioral Research 5: 217-234.

--- (1968) "An approach to multivariate analysis of ordinal data." Amer. Sociological Rev. 33: 171-177.

--- (1964) "Simple measures of association for the triple dichotomy." J. of Royal Stat. Assn. 127: 409-415.

--- (1962) "A new asymmetric measure of association." Amer. Sociological Rev. 27: 799-811.

USLANER, E. (forthcoming) Regression Analysis. Sage University Papers on Quantitative Applications in the Social Sciences. Beverly Hills and London: Sage Pub.

WILSON, T. P. (1974) "Measures of association for bivariate ordinal hypotheses," pp. 327-342 in H. M. Blalock (ed.) Measurement in the Social Sciences. Chicago: Aldine-Atherton.

--- (1970) "Critique of ordinal variables." Social Forces 49: 432-444.

--- (1968) "A proportional-reduction in error interpretation for Kendall's tau-b." Social Forces 47: 340-342.

300.01
H6422

107 94

LINCOLN CHRISTIAN COLLEGE AND SEMINARY

DAVID K. HILDEBRAND is professor of statistics at the Wharton School, University of Pennsylvania. He holds a Ph.D. from Carnegie-Mellon University and has authored several papers, refereed, and reviewed books for many statistics journals, including the Annals of Mathematical Statistics, Econometrica, *and the* American Statistician.

JAMES D. LAING, professor of public policy at the University of Pennsylvania and National Fellow (1976-77) at the Hoover Institution on War, Revolution and Peace, Stanford University, holds a Ph.D. in political science from Stanford University. His interests include research methods, authority systems in formal organizations, coalition behavior, and game theoretic analysis. He is an editor of the Journal of Mathematical Sociology.

HOWARD ROSENTHAL, Roger Williams Straus Professor of Social Sciences at Princeton University, holds a Ph.D. in political science from the Massachussetts Institute of Technology. His current interests include statistical models for scaling roll call voting data, and the analysis of balancing political institutions, partisan politics, divided government, and the macroeconomy.

The three authors have collaborated in presenting various technical papers on research methods in professional conferences and scientific journals. They recently published Prediction Analysis of Cross Classifications *(1977).*

3 4711 00190 4913